MW00679637

Crime Prevention and Security Management

Series editor
Martin Gill
Perpetuity Research
Tunbridge Wells, Kent, United Kingdom

'This is an indispensable book which highlights the ease with which some organised criminals commit fraud, often using professional enablers and frequently making significant profit. The book provides a fascinating and compelling analysis of the national data coupled with offender perspectives on their criminal activity and the criminal justice system; the book also examines the challenges faced by investigators and the often devastating effect organised fraud has on victims. Once and for all, the myth that somehow fraud is a victimless crime is exploded.'

—Mick Creedon, BA, MA, QPM, *Retired Chief Constable and National Policing Lead for Serious and Organised Crime, Financial Crime and Asset Recovery, UK*

It is widely recognized that we live in an increasingly unsafe society, but the study of security and crime prevention has lagged behind in its importance on the political agenda and has not matched the level of public concern. This exciting new series aims to address these issues looking at topics such as crime control, policing, security, theft, workplace violence and crime, fear of crime, civil disorder, white collar crime and anti-social behaviour. International in perspective, providing critically and theoretically-informed work, and edited by a leading scholar in the field, this series will advance new understandings of crime prevention and security management.

More information about this series at
http://www.palgrave.com/series/14928

Tiggey May • Bina Bhardwa

Organised Crime Groups involved in Fraud

palgrave
macmillan

Tiggey May
Institute for Criminal Policy Research
Birkbeck, University of London
London, UK

Bina Bhardwa
Institute for Criminal Policy Research
Birkbeck, University of London
London, UK

Crime Prevention and Security Management
ISBN 978-3-319-69400-9 ISBN 978-3-319-69401-6 (eBook)
https://doi.org/10.1007/978-3-319-69401-6

Library of Congress Control Number: 2017958137

Printed on acid-free paper

This Palgrave Macmillan imprint is published by Springer Nature
The registered company is Springer International Publishing AG
The registered company address is: Gewerbestrasse 11, 6330 Cham, Switzerland

In memory of Daffy, whose love, support, and zest for life knew no boundaries. Tigs

Series Editor's Introduction

This book provides an excellent insight into organised crime, organised fraud, and fraud generally. Tiggey May and Bina Bhardwa will introduce you to the range of problems that plague and undermine the formal response to fraud offences. Via their own original research they provide an important insight into the behaviour of organised offenders, tracing their diverse behaviour in committing a range of offences while remaining determinedly (and largely successfully) under the police radar.

As the authors note, fraud constitutes about a third of all reported offences and the costs are astronomical. What we learn is that those engaged in high-level organised fraud are distinct—at least when compared with other types of organised crime operations—in that they commit an exceptionally high number of offences; facilitate extensive criminality by others; regularly use the services of professional enablers, sometimes blackmailing them into acting corruptly; and overall have a considerable and largely unrecognised impact on local communities.

The authors report on the perspectives of 31 offenders, many of whom they interviewed in prison. They found the majority made a conscious decision to commit offences, attracted by the enormous benefits that can be accrued. You will read about the process by which some offenders are recruited by organised crime groups (OCGs), sometimes by people they knew, including friends, and sometimes by strangers; some were duped, some were bribed, some exploited an opportunity, and some traced their behaviour to a general recklessness or greed. You will read about the ways OCGs are structured and the much discussed existence of a hierarchy including a 'Mr Big' which they find was in evidence.

The criminal justice system is found wanting in many different ways. While the police response to fraud committed by OCGs is complicated by not just the volume of offending but also the complexity of cases (especially when there is an international dimension), they can also be onerous and time consuming to manage; there are 'no quick jobs'. They find that some investigators lack the requisite skills. Attempts to reclaim money obtained illegally are too often unsuccessful or only partially so. As a consequence of all this, success is often judged in being able to curtail offending rather than generate prosecutions. This means some fraudsters are not pursued, including and even especially those who are in the professions and play a crucial role in enabling crime. This may be unpalatable, but it is a consequence of factors that include a low priority to tackling fraud from a range of stakeholders, not just the police.

The authors offer their insights on ways of improving matters including a better use of criminal sanctions, improved intelligence sharing, and promulgating the fact that fraud is not victimless and is in fact a serious offence with serious negative implications for victims.

This is an important study that adds greatly to our understanding of organised fraud and all its implications. At the same time it lays the foundation for thinking more constructively about the response, especially at the local level.

September 2017 Martin Gill

Acknowledgements

We owe an enormous debt of gratitude to our funders, the Dawes Trust. Without their generosity this study would not have been possible. We would also like to express our thanks to Steph Carey and Josie Taylor at Palgrave Macmillan for their editorial assistance, guidance, and patience whilst we prepared our book. The views expressed in this report are, however, those of the authors and not necessarily those of the Dawes Trust or Palgrave Macmillan.

Studies of this nature can only be made possible through the dedication and commitment of many individuals. To preserve the anonymity of our enforcement respondents, we have not thanked by name the many individuals who gave up their time, provided us with important insights into their work, and helped us in numerous other ways during the lifetime of the project. We are, nevertheless, very grateful to them all.

We would like to express particular thanks to Dr Tim McSweeney, who conducted the quantitative analysis of the National Crime Agency's Organised Crime Group Mapping data and wrote up the findings. His skilled statistical analysis was invaluable to the study. We would also like to extend a special thanks to PC Steve Farrer and his colleagues for their intelligence assistance, Chief Superintendent Jim Allen, Detective Chief Inspector Mark Knibbs, Mick Beattie, Mike Nichols, and John Unsworth, whose help with this study we can only describe as a godsend. We would also like to thank Richard Sen, our intern on this study, whose assistance was instrumental in getting us to the finishing line. Colleagues from the Institute for Criminal Policy Research we would like to thank include Dr Jessica Jacobson, Professor Mike Hough, and Gill Hunter for their editorial expertise and comments on earlier drafts, Susan Lea Gerrard for her administrative assistance, and Paul Turnbull for his support throughout the lifetime of the study.

We would also like to extend a special thanks to all the enforcement professionals who agreed to be interviewed, to the NCA for allowing us access to the data they hold on organised crime groups involved in fraud, and to the Ministry of Justice for allowing us access to the Prison Service.

We are also grateful for the invaluable advice and support provided by our Steering Group: our Chair Stephen Webb, Chief Constable Mick Creedon, Chief Superintendent Dave Clarke, Sara Skodbo, Gregor McGill, Rob Street, Tom Bucke, Edward Kleemans, Stuart Kirby, Claire Bentley, Graham Gardner, Sappho Xenakis, and Commissioner Adrian Leppard.

Finally, we would like to give a heartfelt thanks to our offender interviewees for the candour and patience with which they described their activities to us, for their humour and insights, and for giving up their time to take part in this study.

September 2017

Tiggey May
Bina Bhardwa

Contents

Acronyms

ARA	Asset Recovery Agency
ATM	Automated Teller Machine
Cifas	Credit Industry Fraud Avoidance System
CPS	Crown Prosecution Service
DDOS	Distributed Denial of Service
DOS	Denial of Service
FATF	Financial Action Task Force
FCA	Financial Conduct Authority
FRO	Financial Reporting Order
HMIC	Her Majesty's Inspectorate of Constabulary
HMRC	Her Majesty's Revenue and Customs
ICT	Information Communication Technology
LEAs	Law Enforcement Agencies
MoJ	Ministry of Justice
NCA	National Crime Agency
NFA	National Fraud Authority
NFIB	National Fraud Intelligence Bureau
OCGs	Organised Crime Groups
OCGM	Organised Crime Group Mapping
ONS	Office for National Statistics
PCCs	Police and Crime Commissioners
PNC	Police National Computer
PoCA	Proceeds of Crime Act (2002)
ROCUs	Regional Organised Crime Units
SCPO	Serious Crime Prevention Order

SFO	Serious Fraud Office
SOCPA	Serious Organised Crime and Policing Act (2005)
SRA	Solicitors Regulatory Authority
UN	United Nations
UWO	Unexplained Wealth Orders
VAT	Value Added Tax

List of Figures

List of Tables

CHAPTER 1

Introduction

Abstract This chapter outlines the background to the study, including why the research was conducted and the aims and methods of the research. In this chapter the authors highlight how scant our knowledge is on organised criminals involved in fraud, how little we know about pathways into fraud and individual experiences of organised criminality, and how slight our understanding is of how cases come to light, the investigative process, and the challenges faced by law enforcement professionals when investigating organised groups involved in fraud.

Keywords Economic crime • Economic downturn • Financial crisis • Fraud • Technologies

Over the last 25 years, traditional perceptions of organised crime and the types of criminality associated with it have evolved. Drug and firearms trafficking, fraud, cybercrime, organised money laundering, modern slavery, and child sexual exploitation are examples of existing and new threats which have been made easier to commit by the use and exploitation of technologies, transport and communications infrastructure, geopolitical contexts, and existing legitimate business structures—'the drivers of crime'—by organised criminals (Europol 2017a). As a result, this has changed the nature of and the way we view, understand, and respond to

T. May, B. Bhardwa, *Organised Crime Groups involved in Fraud*,
Crime Prevention and Security Management,
https://doi.org/10.1007/978-3-319-69401-6_1

organised crime in the UK and across the globe. This book presents findings from a three-year study on organised crime groups (OCGs) involved in fraud in the UK. Whilst fraud is not a new crime, the scale and sophistication with which it is committed by organised criminals makes it 'the characteristic crime of the twenty-first century' (Albanese 2005) and therefore ripe for further examination.

Organised Crime and Fraud in the UK[1]

In this book, we define organised crime as serious crime planned, coordinated, and conducted by people working together on a continuing basis (definitional issues are considered in more detail in Chap. 2). It is estimated that organised crime costs the UK £20–£40 billion annually (Home Office 2009, 2011). Mills et al. (2013) have reported that the total social and economic cost of organised crime in the UK is around £24 billion a year, of which £8.9 billion is attributed to organised fraud. The 2008 financial crisis and ensuing domestic 'economic downturn' along with the proliferation of new technologies and widespread use of the internet provided OCGs with the fertile ground, ease, methods, and tools to flourish (Home Office 2009, 2013). As a result there has been a surge in economic criminality in the UK (ONS 2016), in particular criminality facilitated by the internet. Cyber-enabled fraud[2] often involves criminal networks operating from overseas and across jurisdictions (National Crime Agency 2015, 2016a). Described as a 'conduit for criminal activity' (Wall 2015), the internet and advances in technology have created new, faster, and easier methods for offenders to commit fraud on an industrial scale (ONS 2016; Cifas 2016). Further, with the re-emergence of what has been termed 'super cases' where the alleged value of the fraud case is £50 million or more,[3] it is unlikely that frauds of this scale and complexity are committed by individuals acting alone. Attracting the attention of OCGs, fraud has become 'one of the most lucrative criminal activities for criminal organisations in Europe' (Savona and Riccardi 2015: 37). In 2013, around 1400 OCGs were involved in economic crime in the UK, many of which were also engaged in other serious and organised crimes (Home Office 2013).

High rewards and the low risk of detection and prosecution make fraud particularly attractive to OCGs.[4] The lowered risks stem from the complexity of fraud investigations, which are further compounded if fraud is committed via the internet and/or require international, cross-border police cooperation.[5] Fraud is typically viewed 'either as the primary activity of an OCG or as an enabler/funding stream for other serious crimes' (National Fraud Authority 2013a, b: 10). The link between organised crime and fraud on a local scale shows a similar picture. One study examining the impact of fraud on local communities in two police force areas in England found that around 31–45% of frauds committed locally were linked to OCGs (Garner et al. 2016).

Successive governments have consequently faced increasing pressure to tackle the threat of organised economic criminality by expanding the capabilities of law enforcement agencies (LEAs) alongside introducing new and strengthening existing legislation. Modelled on the counterterrorism framework, the launch of the *Serious and Organised Crime Strategy* in 2013 under the Coalition (Conservative-Liberal Democrat) government of 2010–15 outlined that UK police forces, directed by Police and Crime Commissioners (PCCs), should work with cross-governmental partners and the public and private sectors to deliver the four strategic objectives of *Pursue*, *Prevent*, *Protect*, and *Prepare*—all of which are aimed at reducing the threat posed by serious and organised crime (Home Office 2013).

Historically, fraud has not been viewed as a policing or government priority (Doig et al. 2001; HM Government 2006). Over the last decade, however, there has been a range of legislative and policy reforms in the UK. Understanding and combating fraud is now firmly on government policy agendas, as is evident from the Fraud Act 2006,[6] the recent inclusion of 'fraud' in the Crime Survey for England and Wales in October 2015 (ONS 2016), amendments to The Proceeds of Crime Act (2002) in 2015 which seek to undermine the financial incentives of crime,[7] and more recently the Criminal Finances Act 2017,[8] in addition to the establishment of the Joint Fraud Taskforce.[9] However, OCGs have proved themselves to be relatively resilient to enforcement efforts. The most recent estimates suggest that there are approximately 5500 OCGs active in the UK, made up of 37,000 individuals (Mills et al. 2013).

Why Focus on Organised Crime and Fraud?

Whilst there is a wealth of knowledge about organised crime and its traditional links with, for example, drugs and firearms, comparatively less is known about organised crime and its links with fraud. Despite fraud being characterised as 'the crime of the century', little is known about OCGs who graduate or shift into fraud, their experiences of committing fraud, and the policing response. In addressing this gap, this book provides a timely contribution to research in this field.

Aims of the Research

As discussed above, there is limited research about organised criminals involved in economic fraud or how fraudsters become embroiled in organised criminality. There is a paucity of literature examining routes into fraud and individual experiences of organised criminality. Whilst the evidence about the policing of organised criminality is widely available, less is known about how cases come to light, the investigative process, and the challenges faced by law enforcement professionals when investigating the organised groups that commit fraud. Drawing on the findings of a multi-method study, this book aims to fill some of these knowledge gaps whilst also adding to the growing body of research and academic evidence on both organised fraudsters and their policing counterparts. The main aim of the research was to establish whether OCGs involved in fraud are becoming more structured, more organised, and more versatile. To achieve this aim the study had three main objectives:

- To assess the offending versatility, at a national level, of known members of OCGs in England and Wales as reflected by the degree of overlap in their criminal records between offences of fraud, money-laundering, drug trafficking, and organised immigration crime;
- To profile the characteristics and criminal careers of those 'polymorphous' offenders who are active across a broad range of illicit activities; and
- To explore OCG offenders' and enforcement professionals' perspectives on the criminal justice system and its efforts to tackle organised crime and fraud.

To achieve these objectives the research had two distinct phases:

- Phase 1: An in-depth quantitative analysis of the data held by the NCA on OCGs involved in fraud.
- Phase 2: A qualitative analysis of OCGs involved in fraud through interviews with offenders and enforcement professionals.

The two phases sought to answer the following questions:

- How do the characteristics of known OCGs involved in fraud-related offences differ from other offenders?
- What are the routes into fraud and organised crime?
- How serious a threat to OCG activity do offenders perceive LEAs to be?
- What are the tactics and strategies employed by LEAs to detect and apprehend offenders and disrupt OCGs?
- How do LEAs operate and co-operate at local, regional, national, and international levels to prevent, detect, disrupt, and apprehend individuals and groups?

Methods

This was a challenging study, and to our knowledge no UK research into OCGs involved in economic fraud on this scale has been attempted before. The basic approach was simple: analyse the national data held on OCGs involved in fraud and get known members of OCGs involved in fraud to talk about their past activities in a setting—prison—where they have nothing to lose by being honest. In practical terms, there were many obstacles to achieving this aim, including securing access to individuals, securing access to data on criminal histories, and persuading offenders and LEA staff to take part in the research. A combination of quantitative and qualitative research methods was employed to answer the research questions set out above. The study had the following core elements:

- Linkage and analysis of existing administrative datasets held by the NCA, 'mining' them for information about criminal careers to obtain a national enforcement picture on OCGs involved in fraud;
- Thirty-one depth interviews with convicted members of OCGs involved in fraud;
- Forty interviews with enforcement professionals and four interviews with key stakeholders.

Limitations of the Research

No single study could provide a definitive view of the structure, nature, and capabilities of OCGs involved in fraud, and this study is no exception. However, as far as we know, this study is the most comprehensive analysis of organised economic fraudsters to have been undertaken in the UK. As part of the study we have analysed a large dataset provided to us by the NCA and conducted in-depth interviews with a large sample of organised. We examined organised criminals involved in economic fraud, including mortgage fraud, investment fraud, distribution fraud, money laundering, customs and revenue fraud, insurance fraud, and trader fraud.[10] Whilst we looked at cyber-enabled fraud (conducted both online and offline), a notable exclusion from this study was cyber-dependent fraud. We excluded cyber-dependent fraud for two reasons: firstly, whilst cyber-dependent fraud is not new, at the time of research there were few convictions linked to organised criminal networks. Having only a small pool of potential offenders to invite for an interview was viewed as problematic. Secondly, cyber-dependent fraudsters commit very different types of offences (e.g. illicit intrusions into computer networks, such as hacking; and the disruption or downgrading of computer functionality and network space, such as malware and Denial of Service (DOS) or Distributed Denial of Service (DDOS) attacks[11]), compared to cyber-enabled or paper-based fraudsters. Including cyber-dependent fraud in the study would have made comparisons and generalisations to offline fraud or cyber-enabled fraud difficult.

Contextually, this research was carried out about five years after the Global Financial Crisis of 2008,[12] which had, and continues to have, a marked impact on the UK economy. As a result, the economic crimes discussed in this book are a reflection of the *types* of crime being uncovered by or reported to the police during this period. The fast-evolving nature of fraud and organised crime suggests that almost ten years on from the 'Great Recession', the picture is likely to be somewhat different.

Uniquely, this study provides new insights into the routes in, experiences of, and views on organised criminality from the perspectives of organised fraudsters, as well as highlighting the challenges and problems associated with policing this type of criminal. Our qualitative findings rely on the honesty and accuracy of our interviewees. The offenders we interviewed were, of course, all convicted of offences of dishonesty, and it is reasonable to suspect that some will have been less than honest with us. However, it is worth stressing that whilst almost all were serving prison sentences, they all agreed to be interviewed and most had little or nothing to lose by being honest with us. Our impression was, and remains, that they responded positively to researchers who were genuinely interested in hearing about their 'craft'. Some of them had, nevertheless, inflicted serious harm on their victims, and it was clear that they had a range of strategies for self-justification; some clearly took a lot of trouble to present themselves to us in the best possible light. Readers must obviously bear this in mind when weighing up our findings.

We are confident that our findings are internally valid. We listened to our interviewees carefully and with appropriate scepticism, challenging accounts where appropriate. However, as with many qualitative studies, there are clear limits to the external validity or generalisability of our findings, as our samples of enforcement professionals and convicted offenders cannot claim to be fully representative. Despite any limitations, we hope our work acts as an important contribution to the field of organised crime and fraud research.

Structure of This Book

Chapter 2 examines the existing literature and what it tells us about organised crime and fraud. It explores the historically contested definitions of organised crime, outlines the definition adopted for this book, and presents views on the extent of the 'threat' posed by OCGs. Further, it looks at the scale of fraud in the UK and the policing response. The chapter concludes with an overview of what the data from the NCA tell us about economic organised fraudsters, providing the reader with a national picture of what the police know about OCGs involved in fraud. Chapter 3 examines the routes into organised crime and the crime of fraud from the perspective of our offender interviewees. Chapter 4 looks at the structure of OCGs, drawing on the analysis from our offender interviews. It provides an insight into the fluidity of OCGs and the impact of social, business, and professional networks on criminal activity. Chapter 5 discusses and highlights the challenges faced by enforcement professionals when policing organised crime and fraud and the views of both offenders and police officers of the court process. Finally, Chap. 6 presents a summary of our findings and our concluding thoughts.

Notes

1. This book presents empirical data from England and Wales and literature from the UK, Europe, and English-speaking nations.
2. The National Crime Agency (NCA) defines cyber-dependent and cyber-enabled as follows: 'Cyber-dependent crimes can only be committed using computers, computer networks or other forms of information communication technology (ICT). They include the creation and spread of malware

for financial gain, hacking to steal sensitive personal or industry data and denial of service attacks to cause reputational damage. Cyber-enabled crimes, such as fraud, the purchasing of illegal drugs and child sexual exploitation, can be conducted on or offline, but online may take place at unprecedented scale and speed.' NCA (2016b) Strategic Cyber Industry Group: Cyber Crime Assessment 2016. *Need for a stronger law enforcement and business partnership to fight cyber crime* 2016.

3. KPMG (2017) https://home.kpmg.com/uk/en/home/insights/2017/01/uk-fraud-value-reaches-1bn-first-time-five-years.html.
4. Europol (2017b) https://www.europol.europa.eu/crime-areas-and-trends/crime-areas/economic-crime.
5. Europol (2017b) https://www.europol.europa.eu/crime-areas-and-trends/crime-areas/economic-crime.
6. The Fraud Act 2006 categorised fraud into three primary offences: fraud by false representation; fraud by failing to disclose information; and fraud by abuse of position. See: http://www.legislation.gov.uk/ukpga/2006/35/crossheading/fraud.
7. The Serious Crime Act 2015 made amendments to PoCA 2002 relating to the confiscation of criminal assets. See: http://www.legislation.gov.uk/ukpga/2015/9/contents/enacted.
8. The Act now gives LEAs the power to recover proceeds of crime, tackle money laundering, tax evasion, corruption, and counterterrorist financing. See: http://services.parliament.uk/bills/2016-17/criminalfinances.html.
9. Set up in February 2016, the Joint Fraud Taskforce involves collaboration between government, LEAs, and the banks in the collective fight against fraud. Representatives on the Taskforce include City of London Police, the NCA, Cifas, and the Bank of England, to name a few.
10. For definitions of the types of fraud covered in this book, please see the Glossary.
11. The definition of cyber-dependent fraud is from the Crown Prosecution Service website. http://www.cps.gov.uk/legal/a_to_c/cybercrime/#a03.
12. For further information on the Global Financial Crisis, see Financial Times (2017) https://www.ft.com/global-financial-crisis.

References

Albanese, J. (2005). Fraud: The Characteristic Crime of the 21st Century. *Trends in Organized Crime, 8*(4), 6–14.

Cifas. (2016). *Fraudscape 2016.* London: Cifas.

Doig, A., Johnson, S., & Levi, M. (2001). New Public Management, Old Populism and the Policing of Fraud. *Public Policy and Administration, 16*, 9.

Europol. (2017a). EU Serious and Organised Crime Threat Assessment: Crime in the Age of Technology. *Europol* [Online]. Available at: https://www.europol.europa.eu/newsroom/news/crime-in-age-of-technology-%E2%80%93-europol%E2%80%99s-serious-and-organised-crime-threat-assessment-2017. Accessed 26 Apr 2017.

Europol. (2017b). Economic Crime. *Europol* [Online]. Available at: https://www.europol.europa.eu/crime-areas-and-trends/crime-areas/economic-crime. Accessed 26 Apr 2017.

Financial Times. (2017). Global Financial Crisis. *Financial Times* [Online]. Available at: https://www.ft.com/global-financial-crisis. Accessed 26 Apr 2017.

Garner, S., Crocker, R., Skidmore, M., Webb, S., Graham, J., & Gill, M. (2016). *Reducing the Impact of Serious Organised Crime in Local Communities: Organised Fraud in Local Communities* (Briefing 1). Perpetuity Research and the Police Foundation. Available at: http://www.police-foundation.org.uk/uploads/holding/projects/org_fraud_in_local_communities_final.pdf

HM Government. (2006). *Fraud Review: Final Report.* London: Home Office.

Home Office. (2009). *Extending Our Reach: A Comprehensive Approach to Tackling Organised Crime.* London: The Stationery Office.

Home Office. (2011). *Local to Global: Reducing the Risk from Organised Crime.* London: Home Office.

Home Office. (2013). *Serious and Organised Crime Strategy.* London: Home Office.

KPMG. (2017, January 24). Value of UK Fraud Breaks £1 Billion Barrier for the First Time in Five Years. *KPMG* [Online]. Available at: https://home.kpmg.com/uk/en/home/insights/2017/01/uk-fraud-value-reaches-1bn-first-time-five-years.html. Accessed 10 May 2017.

Mills, H., Skodbo, S., and Blyth, P. (2013). *Understanding Organised Crime: Estimating the Scale and the Social and Economic Costs* (Research Report 73). London: Home Office.

National Fraud Authority. (2013a). *Annual Fraud Indicator.* Available at: https://www.gov.uk/government/uploads/system/uploads/attachment_data/file/206552/nfa-annual-fraud-indicator-2013.pdf

National Fraud Authority. (2013b). *Fighting Fraud Together, Quarterly Update—April 2013.* London: Home Office.

NCA. (2015). *National Strategic Assessment of Serious and Organised Crime 2015.* National Crime Agency.

NCA. (2016a). *National Strategic Assessment of Serious and Organised Crime 2016.* National Crime Agency.

NCA. (2016b). Strategic Cyber Industry Group: Cyber Crime Assessment 2016. *Need for a Stronger Law Enforcement and Business Partnership to Fight Cyber Crime 2016*. National Crime Agency.

ONS. (2016). Overview of Fraud Statistics: Year Ending Mar 2016. *Office of National Statistics* [Online]. Available at: https://www.ons.gov.uk/peoplepopulationandcommunity/crimeandjustice/articles/overviewoffraudstatistics/yearendingmarch2016. Accessed 26 Apr 2017.

Savona, E. U., & Riccardi, M. (2015). *From Illegal Markets to Legitimate Businesses: The Portfolio of Organised Crime in Europe*. Trento: Transcrime–Università degli Studi di Trento.

Wall, D. S. (2015). The Internet as a Conduit for Criminals. In A. Pattavina (Ed.), *Information Technology and the Criminal Justice System* (pp. 77–98). Thousand Oaks: Sage.

CHAPTER 2

What Do We Know About Organised Crime and Fraud?

Abstract This chapter examines the existing academic literature and what it tells us about organised crime and fraud, both at a national and an international level. With a traditional focus from enforcement on organised crime groups (OCGs) involved in drugs and firearms, it is argued that comparatively little is known about OCGs involved in fraud. This imbalance is reflected in the paucity of empirical research in this area, although this picture is slowly changing. This chapter explores the historically contested definitions of organised crime, outlines the definition adopted in this book, and presents views on the extent of the 'threat' posed by OCGs. Further, it looks at the scale of fraud in the UK and the policing response. The chapter concludes with a national overview of what the OCG mapping data, held by the National Crime Agency (NCA) in the UK, tells us about economic organised fraudsters.

Keywords Organised crime • Policing • Alien conspiracy theory • The Fraud Act 2006 • Organised Crime Group Mapping (OCGM) data • Intent and capability

This chapter explores what the available research literature tells us about organised crime and fraud. It starts with definitional issues, and then examines the extent of fraud in the UK. We go on to explore the current

T. May, B. Bhardwa, *Organised Crime Groups involved in Fraud*, Crime Prevention and Security Management, https://doi.org/10.1007/978-3-319-69401-6_2

law enforcement response to the threat of organised crime and fraud at a national, regional, and local level. The existing research literature tends to treat the topics of 'organised crime' and 'fraud' as separate and unrelated, and pays little attention to the increasingly symbiotic relationship between the two—a research gap this book intends to fill. We conclude the chapter by presenting our analysis of the Organised Crime Group Mapping (OCGM) data, held by the National Crime Agency (NCA). These data provide an outline of what is currently known about OCGs involved in fraud at a national level in England and Wales.

What Is Organised Crime?

'Organised crime' remains a contested concept (Levi 2012; Finckenauer 2005). Much of the academic literature on the subject of organised crime is concerned with its definition. Wright states that 'unfortunately, the official documentation and the critical literature set out almost as many definitions as there are people with an interest in the subject' (2006: 2–3). Part of the difficulty of defining 'organised crime' lies in the fact that the term can apply to:

1) the organisation of crime (e.g. crimes that involve a degree of pre-planning and preparation), or
2) the organisation of offenders (e.g. how offenders come together and how these long-standing or fleeting social relations shape OCGs), or
3) the structures of power and accountability established by some OCGs (as exemplified by the symbolism and power related to the Sicilian Mafiosi) (von Lampe 2015).

Thus some OCGs can lack structure whilst remaining well-organised, and others can be very disorganised despite clear structures. In the absence of a legal definition in England and Wales (Home Office 2013) and in other parts of the world, numerous definitions have been put forward by politicians, law enforcement agencies, and academics; von Lampe (2017) has identified over 190 definitions of 'organised crime'. Some commentators have said that the very ambiguity and malleability of the concept of 'organised crime' is politically useful as it can be used to shape public opinion and to direct police resources (van Dijck 2007; von Lampe 2015; Edwards and Levi 2008).

Some writers question whether traditional definitions of organised crime are able to capture the complexities of cybercrime (Grabosky 2013), whilst others suggest that the scholarly quest for a unified definition of organised crime is a futile one (van Dijck 2007). Instead, given the plethora of definitions and the 'arbitrary' line between what constitutes organised crime and what does not, von Lampe (2015) suggests that it may be more useful for those studying organised crime to add to the definitional debate as an *outcome* of their study, instead of seeking to pin down a single, catch-all definition from the *outset* of a study.

Definitions of Organised Crime

Regardless of the number of definitions, there appears to be a consensus that the concept of organised crime (von Lampe 2015; Hobbs 2013) entered popular discourse in the 1920s, originating in the United States and centred mainly on the study of familial and kinship groups such as 'the Mafia' (Paoli 2003; Wright 2006). The term was adopted in Europe from the 1960s and 1970s and became used globally from the 1990s onwards, 'exported like a criminal justice version of Starbucks' (Hobbs 2013: 12). Amplified in the news media and through films such as *The Godfather*, 'the Mafia' has become synonymous with the concept of organised crime across the globe (Finckenauer 2005; Levi 2012; Lavorgna et al. 2013). However, Finckenauer (2005) warns of the dangers for policy and practice of equating organised crime with social constructions of 'the Mafia', which, he argues, diverts attention from the variable manifestations of organised crime.

The United Nations (1976) defined organised crime as:

> *...the large-scale and complex criminal activity carried out by groups of persons, however loosely or tightly organized, for the enrichment of those participating and at the expense of the community and its members; it is frequently accomplished through ruthless disregard of any law, including offences against the person, and frequently in connection with political corruption* (cited in Wright 2006: 8).

However, the most cited definition of organised crime comes from the Council of Europe (1997), which proposed that four criteria must all be met if crime is to be considered 'organised':

1) collaboration of three or more people;
2) for a prolonged or indefinite period of time;
3) suspected or convicted of committing serious criminal offences; and
4) with the objective of pursuing profit and/power (cited in Finckenauer 2005: 70).

The Council of Europe (1997) definition was also echoed by the United Nations (UN) *Convention against Transnational Organized Crime* (2000), which defined an OCG as 'a structured group of three or more persons, existing for a period of time and acting in concert with the aim of committing one or more serious crimes or offences established in accordance with this Convention, in order to obtain, directly or indirectly, a financial or other material benefit' (cited in Wright 2006: 9).

More recently, the definition has been adapted in the UK's 2013 *Serious and Organised Crime Strategy*:

> *...serious crime planned, coordinated and conducted by people working together on a continuing basis. Their motivation is often, but not always, financial gain* (Home Office 2013: 14).

In our view this definition is simple and clear, whilst remaining inclusive, and it is the one that we have adopted for this book. Of course, within such a broad definition sub-categories of organised crime can be identified. In particular, the literature indicates how certain political contexts, conflict zones, or 'failed' or corrupt states provide fertile ground for OCGs to flourish. Political instability presents opportunities which are exploited by OCGs. Conditions in Italy, Eastern Europe, and China feature prominently in the research literature. Arguably, terrorist groups fall within our definition, though some commentators would not treat as OCGs those whose motivation is to achieve political change (Finckenauer 2005).

Edwards and Levi (2008) discuss the organisation of serious crime, refocusing our attention to the way in which crimes are *organized* rather than looking at the composition of the group. The need to reconceptualise the term was noted as early on as the 1970s, with Cohen (1977) subtly twisting the concept of organised crime to criminal organisation, arguing that all crimes require a degree of organisation and little is carried out by individuals working alone. Understanding the nature of organised crime requires an understanding of the criminal activities undertaken, the structural and relational dynamics between criminals, and the governance of criminal groups (von Lampe 2015).

The Perceived 'Threat' of Organised Crime

Against a backdrop of growing pressure on governments in the UK and European Union (EU) to tackle the threat of organised crime and the introduction of increased policing powers and resources to do so, a detailed understanding of the nature and scope of the threat posed by organised crime has remained elusive (Edwards and Levi 2008: 364; Sproat 2009, 2012). Organised offenders variously operate within national and across international boundaries. However, it has been argued that the 'media, police and politicians unwittingly or cynically exaggerate some transnational threats and the prospective effect of their proposed remedies' (Levi 2012: 599). A recurring theme in the literature is the historical framing of organised crime as an external threat to liberal democracies (Edwards and Levi 2008). This 'alien conspiracy theory' emanates from the United States in the 1950s and refers to the perceived threat from (usually) ethnic minority 'outsider' groups (Edwards 2004; Morselli et al. 2011; Levi 2012). Historically, in the UK, this has translated into fears surrounding 'Jamaican Yardies, Turkish heroin traffickers and Balkan, especially Albanian, traffickers in the sex industry', which have resulted in increased enforcement activity against these groups (Edwards 2004: 31). Critiquing 'the alien conspiracy theory', a number of studies have highlighted the need to examine the local manifestation of organised crime (Hobbs 1998, 2013; Garner et al. 2016).

What Is Fraud?

Fraud is 'when trickery is used to gain a dishonest advantage, which is often financial, over another person'.[1] Using the Home Office Counting Rules for Recorded Crime (2017), the National Fraud Intelligence Bureau (NFIB) record 62 'types' of fraud offence, ranging from dating scams, ticket fraud, and pyramid or ponzi schemes to computer misuse crime and hacking offences.[2, 3] In English Criminal Law, the Fraud Act 2006 created three primary offences for fraud, each punishable with a maximum prison sentence of up to ten years:

1) fraud by false representation;
2) fraud by failing to disclose information;
3) fraud by abuse of position

As the Fraud Act 2006 passed through parliament awaiting Royal Assent, questions were raised as to whether the Act would be able to 'get the law right'. It was suggested that fraud historically has suffered from an association with white-collar criminality committed by the 'respectable classes' or the outcome of what was viewed as 'respectable opportunism' as opposed to other criminal acts that are committed by the 'dangerous' 'criminal' classes in society, and this has therefore shaped public attitudes towards fraud as a 'lesser crime' (Wilson and Wilson 2007).

Careers in Organised Crime and Fraud

Research examining the criminal trajectories of individuals involved in organised crime indicates that, overall, those involved in organised criminality tend to be older than non-OCG criminals, have few previous convictions, have no known prior criminal involvement, and often have a legitimate job. These findings obviously present challenges to traditional life-course, criminal career explanations of offending behaviour (Kleemans and de Poot 2008; van Koppen et al. 2010; van Koppen and de Poot 2013). However, more recent research conducted by Francis et al. (2013) found that organised criminals when compared to general offenders had an average of nine criminal sanctions prior to their first organised crime conviction. Kleemans and de Poot (2008) also noted that many who become involved in organised crime are recruited due to their specialist, technical knowledge about a specific field. 'Many actions require specific skills or experiences, and not everyone will have the opportunity to join a crime group' (van Koppen and de Poot 2013: 75–6). As Grabosky states, 'many of those criminals currently operating in cyberspace, alone or within organisations, were competent technicians before turning to crime' (2013: 23).

In 2016 an estimated 3.8 million incidents of fraud were recorded in England and Wales,[4] a rise of 3% from the previous year and accounting for a third of the 11.8 million incidents of crime reported in the same period (Office for National Statistics [ONS], September 2016a, b). With losses amounting to just over £193 billion (private sector fraud £144 billion;

public sector fraud £37.5 billion; individuals £10 billion; charity sector £1.9 billion), fraud poses a sizeable threat to both individuals and businesses in the UK (Button et al. 2016). The social and economic cost of organised crime is estimated to be around £24 billion a year, of which £8.9 billion is attributed to organised fraud (Mills et al. 2013). Globally, the estimated cost of fraud, based on findings from 46 organisations across nine countries, amounts to £7.22 trillion per year (Gee and Button 2013). However, the full extent of fraud is unknown. Measuring fraud is a fraught task for a number of reasons, including the lack of robust methodology and no uniform way of defining 'what counts' as fraud across organisations, fraud that is unreported, where the victim is unaware that they have been defrauded, and the result of organisations labelling incidents of fraud as 'bad debt' (HM Government 2006: 5; Levi and Burrows 2008; Cifas 2016). That said, with the inclusion of fraud in the Crime Survey for England and Wales in 2015 and industry and academic collaborations improving our understanding of the scale of fraud in the UK (e.g. the Annual Fraud Indicator (2016) produced by Experian, PKF Littlejohn, and the University of Portsmouth's Centre for Counter Fraud Studies[5]), the statistical insights into fraud are better than what we have had previously.

Advances in technology and globalisation have changed how money is owned, moved, and stored, which makes fraud in the electronic age 'an easier, more profitable, and less risky way to steal in the twenty-first century' (Albanese 2005: 13). Fraudsters are increasingly more organised, equipped with the technical 'know-how', and able to operate across geographical borders (National Fraud Authority 2011). However, despite the growing popularity of fraud as a crime of choice and its links to other serious crimes such as human trafficking and terrorism (National Fraud Authority 2013a, b; Albanese 2005), fraud has received relatively limited academic attention. In part, this may be because fraud is often viewed as a low political and police priority when compared to other crime problems (Levi 2008: 390; Button et al. 2007).

Fighting Fraud Together 2011 was the strategic plan by the now disbanded National Fraud Authority (2011), which asserted that 'by 2015 our country will be demonstrably more resilient to and less damaged by fraud' (p. 17). To achieve this, along with calls for further cross-sector partnership working, better intelligence information, and good practice-sharing processes, three strategic objectives were identified:

1) raising awareness of fraud (in particular, amongst vulnerable groups),
2) putting in place preventative measures, and
3) targeted enforcement (National Fraud Authority 2011).

Despite the policing and legislative progress that has been achieved (e.g. the introduction of new legislation aimed at curbing fraudulent activity and protecting victims and the inception of Action Fraud), research has shown that fraud offences remain underreported and—where they have been reported—only a small number result in a criminal conviction (National Fraud Authority 2011: 16). For example, of 145,841 frauds reported to and recorded by the police in England and Wales in 2010/11, only 24% resulted in a criminal conviction (ibid.).

Government and Law Enforcement Responses to Organised Crime and Fraud

As mentioned in Chap. 1, various government strategies and associated legislation have been introduced over the years aimed at disrupting organised crime, including

- **Local to Global: Reducing the Risk from Organised Crime (2011):** The aim of this strategy was to set common objectives and a clear line of accountability for those agencies working to combat organised criminality. The strategy emphasised preventative and self-protection work, alongside a focus on enforcement. It established a basis for enhanced international cooperation and improved intelligence gathering and analysis. The strategy also signalled that a new body, the NCA, was to become operational in 2013, with the remit of fighting serious and organised crime.
- **Serious and organised crime strategy (2013):** This strategy was established as a cross-government strategy (not just a Home Office strategy). The strategy launched the NCA, and stated that the aim of the agency would be to target national and international serious and organised criminals and groups. To strengthen the response at a local level the Home Secretary announced that targets were to be removed and accountability increased through Police and Crime Commissioners. The strategy introduced the four P's (Pursue, Prevent, Protect, Prepare) aimed at reducing the threat of serious and organised crime.

- **Serious Crime Act 2015[6]:** This Act included amendments to the Proceeds of Crime Act. In addition, Part 3 section 45 of the 2015 Act set out the offence of participating in the criminal activities of an organised crime group.
- **Criminal Finances Act (2017):** The Criminal Finances Act 2017 becomes law this summer (2017). The legislation represents the most extensive reform of asset confiscation and the anti-money-laundering legislation since the Proceeds of Crime Act was passed in 2002. Investigating authorities have been provided with additional powers which now allow them to compel those under investigation to provide explanations as to the source of their wealth and, where appropriate, confiscate assets/money. The Act also introduced Unexplained Wealth Orders (UWOs) and new measures such as interim freezing orders, extended suspension periods, voluntary information sharing, and joint disclosure reports. In addition, the Act introduced a new criminal offence directed at companies and partnerships where tax evasion is committed by those associated with the company.

Policing Fraud

The policing of fraud extends beyond the work of the police. A patchwork of public, private, and voluntary sector, counter fraud entities are all involved in investigating and prosecuting fraud (Button 2011). This includes the Department for Work and Pensions (which has the largest fraud policing capability), local authorities, the Serious Fraud Office (SFO), the NCA, the Financial Crime Authority, and a department within the National Health Service, to name but a few (Button et al. 2015). The Fraud Review highlighted that a range of organisations involved in policing fraud was essential as 'police knowledge does not present a complete picture of fraudulent activity, and must be complemented by the information held by other organisations such as government departments, local authorities and also the private sector, in order to develop a detailed picture of what is happening' (HM Government 2006: 63). However, the organisational capacity and capabilities of these counter fraud entities to investigate fraud varies considerably and has been described as a 'flawed architecture' (Button 2011). Within some of the organisations, the responsibility for investigating fraud falls within the remit of generalist staff, whilst others have staff tasked specifically with investigating fraud (ibid.).

At a National Level

In response to what was viewed as an uncoordinated police response to fraud (HM Government 2006), the NCA was launched in 2013; the organisation was tasked with coordinating the national response to serious and organised crime. The NCA has four command units each responsible for a different but overlapping area of threat; the responsibility for fraud investigations falls under the Economic Crime Command within the NCA. The four commands are:

1) Organised crime
2) Economic crime
3) Border policing
4) Child exploitation and online protection[7]

Created under the Criminal Justice Act 1987 and established in 1988, the SFO is a government department, funded by the Treasury, set up to tackle high-value, serious, and complex fraud, corruption, and bribery cases.[8] The SFO has 35 cases currently listed as under investigation, awaiting a court hearing, or recently concluded. Cases currently being examined by the SFO range from a self-referral from the Bank of England regarding liquidity auctions to a criminal investigation into an alleged fraudulent investment scheme marketed by Ethical Forestry Limited. Cases referred to or initiated by the SFO tend to be complex and usually involve a lengthy investigative process.

The City of London Police as the national lead police force for fraud hosts the national reporting centre—Action Fraud. All complaints of fraud must, at some point, be reported to Action Fraud. After a case has been reported by the victim, a police officer or agencies such as the Credit Industry Fraud Avoidance System, more commonly known as just Cifas, it is assessed by the NFIB. The NFIB will collate all the available information and if appropriate develop an intelligence package to then send to the most appropriate force to investigate. Once allocated to a force, the investigation will then be allocated to a team. However, with Action Fraud, many local forces are of the view that reports of fraud are not their responsibility, and there remains a need for a coherent and coordinated local response to fraud (Fraud Advisory Panel 2016).

Regional and Local

There are ten Regional Organised Crime Units (ROCUs) in England and Wales, each of which is responsible for leading the regional criminal investigations of three to six local police forces. The aim of the ROCUs is to provide a link between the NCA, City of London Police (as the national lead), and local policing; in essence, the ROCUs are an important part of the national policing network and act as a bridge between the national and local response (HMIC 2015: 13). ROCUs provide local police forces with specialist capabilities (such as surveillance and cybercrime expertise) to assist local forces to disrupt serious and organised crime. However, a recent Her Majesty's Inspectorate of Constabulary (HMIC) report concluded that whilst ROCU capabilities were particularly effective at disrupting the more traditional threats such as drugs, firearms, and money laundering, their response was inconsistent and underdeveloped to new threats such as cybercrime and human trafficking. For local forces to be able to exploit the expertise and specialist skills of ROCU officers, HMIC has recommended that training for these officers needs to be up-to-date, relevant, and regular. By 2015 all ten ROCUs had the capacity and capability to investigate fraud committed by organised criminals.

It is argued that 'despite these many developments at the national and regional level, it is recognised that the key role in the policing of fraud is played at the local level' (City of London Police 2015: 1). Police forces appear to be in the situation where there is an 'imbalance between the over-supply of [fraud] intelligence packages and the more limited operational capacity to act on them' (Doig and Levi 2013: 148). At a local level there has been an overall decline in the number of specialist officers dedicated to investigating fraud and economic crime, which has led to calls for a national fraud police. Button et al. (2015), using Freedom of Information requests sent to the 43 police forces in the UK, found that the need for specialist fraud investigations within the police service was greater than had previously been considered. In addition, he found that this gap appeared to be being filled by a growing number of civilian counter fraud investigators. These investigators were often retired detectives who had previously worked within local or regional fraud units (Button et al. 2007: 193; HM Government 2006).

Research has shown that the majority of police forces in the UK have dedicated fraud departments; however, investigative efforts have tended to focus on asset recovery and fraud cases linked to organised crime over the high-volume, low-value cases (Gannon and Doig 2010; Doig and Levi 2013). Moreover, it is suggested that law enforcement is largely reactive to innovative offending methods, and that it is 'only after losses are incurred that improvements are implemented to reduce (or at least change) criminal opportunities' (Albanese 2005: 12).

The National Picture: Analysis of the NCA-Administered OCGM Data[9]

The OCGM process is described by the NCA as:

> …a process where UK law enforcement agencies collate and share information in a systematic way to aggregate an overall picture of serious and organised crime affecting the UK[10] (NCA 2013).

In June 2014 the NCA provided us with an anonymised extract of data derived from the OCGM process. The data were extracted from returns made by forces and organisations across England, Wales, and Northern Ireland and related to 7448 OCGs.[11] Our analysis, however, was restricted to data relating to 4824 OCGs, comprising slightly more than 33,000 individuals (or nominals) mapped by agencies in England, Wales, and Northern Ireland; 34% of these criminal enterprises were involved in fraud-related activities. Our analysis examined the characteristics of those groups considered to be engaged in high levels of fraud-related criminality (7%), relative to other (low or medium criminality) fraud groups (27%) and all other (non-fraud) OCGs (66%); our findings are presented by these groupings. Our analysis included both active (83%) and archived (17%) cases.

Definitions

For the purpose of our quantitative analysis we have defined fraudsters as those OCGs engaged in current or historic forms of criminality (to a low, medium, or high level) linked to one of over 50 economic crimes recorded via the OCGM mapping process.[12] Following advice from analysts at the NCA, additional frauds relating to commodity importation, counterfeiting or illegal supply, and organised immigration crime and human trafficking (not for sexual exploitation) were also included within our definition.[13]

The Characteristics of Fraud OCGs

Whilst there was no difference between fraud OCGs and others in terms of the average number of known members operating within these groups, they tended to have proportionally fewer men, be of an older average age, and were less likely to be British nationals. As we shall see in Chap. 3, whilst the demographic profile of our qualitative sample broadly replicated that of the profile of organised fraudsters derived from the NCA mapping process, the qualitative sample differed markedly on nationality.

Intent and Capability

Fraud OCGs were considered to have intent and capability across a wider range of areas, including in relation to expertise, infiltration, corruption and subversion, involvement in multiple enterprises, resistance and/or resilience, and cash flow. By contrast, they were less likely to display violent capability, have links with other OCGs, or be considered tactically aware. Those engaged in high levels of fraud-related OCGs were considered to have intent and capability across a larger number of areas, in particular with regard to infiltration, corruption, and subversion, growth potential, expertise, resistance/resilience, involvement in multiple enterprises, and cash flow. They were, however, significantly less likely to display violent capability relative to other (low/medium criminality) fraud groups.

Nature and Extent of Harm

When compared to other criminal enterprises, fraud-related OCGs were significantly more likely to be reported as having:

- an exceptional level of criminality
- a pivotal role in enabling substantial criminality among other OCGs
- some criminal activities not being assessed
- political/reputational damage arising from their activities; and
- impact upon a community to an exceptional level

These differences were largely driven by those groups that were engaged in high levels of fraud-related criminality. In contrast to other fraud-related groups, these particular criminal enterprises were considered to be engaged in an exceptional level of criminality; play a pivotal role in enabling substantial criminality among other groups; had potential for considerable political/ reputational damage arising from their offending; and had key elements of their offending unassessed using the current mapping framework.

Links with Business

OCGs involved in fraud appeared to have more links with other companies and were more likely than other OCGs to be linked to them in the capacity of owner, manager, or other employee. The legitimate companies to which fraud-related criminal enterprises were linked were also significantly more likely to be complicit in facilitating serious crime, laundering, and acting as a front to import/export goods. Those engaged in high levels of fraud-related criminality had links with more companies than other (low/medium criminality) fraud OCGs. Compared to other fraud OCGs, the legitimate companies to which these high criminality fraud groups had links were significantly more likely to be acting as a front to import/export goods and to be complicit in laundering and facilitating serious crime.

Fraud OCGs were more likely to have an identifiable link with business, in particular professional services and other (unspecified) sectors. Conversely, they were less likely to have links with the catering and health/ beauty sectors. Those engaged in high levels of fraud-related criminality were significantly more likely to be linked with other (unspecified) business sectors than other fraud-related OCGs, but less likely to have links with the environmental sector.

Specialist Roles: The Use of Professional Enablers

Fraud OCGs were more likely to incorporate professional enablers within their structure, that is, a regulated occupation or specialist role, and to have more of these specialist roles present within their groups. Regulated occupations were also more likely to be reported within those groups engaged in high levels of fraud-related criminality, in contrast to other fraud groups, and they had more specialist roles present within them.

Technology as an Enabler of Criminality

OCGs involved in fraud were significantly more likely to use technological services for criminal purposes or to enable involvement in crime, to use the internet as an enabler, and to be engaged in a specific internet- or technology-enabled crime type compared to non-fraud OCGs. Those groups involved in a high level of fraud-related criminality were more likely to exploit technological services for criminal purposes or to facilitate involvement in crime, and use the internet as an enabler.

International Connections

Criminal enterprises mapped as having high levels of fraud-related criminality were significantly more likely to have an international dimension and be expanding their enterprises through UK borders, be considered to have a recognised structure, and have estimated assets in excess of £1 million.

In Summary

The key features which distinguished OCGs engaged in a high level of fraud-related criminality from others were:

- having estimated assets in excess of £1 million
- generating significant political/reputational damage arising from their activities
- having an international dimension
- using technology for criminal purposes
- having a regulated occupation within their ranks
- an identifiable link with the business sector
- playing a pivotal role in enabling substantial criminality among other OCGs; and
- involvement in other areas of criminality.

Notes

1. Action Fraud (2017) http://www.actionfraud.police.uk/what-is-fraud.
2. Home Office Counting Rules for Recorded Crime (2017): https://www.gov.uk/government/uploads/system/uploads/attachment_data/file/602811/count-fraud-apr-2017.pdf.
3. See Glossary for definitions of fraud types.
4. ONS (2016b) https://www.ons.gov.uk/peoplepopulationandcommunity/crimeandjustice/bulletins/crimeinenglandandwales/yearendingsept2016#main-points.

5. Button et al. (2016) http://www.port.ac.uk/media/contacts-and-departments/icjs/ccfs/Annual-Fraud-Indicator-2016.pdf.
6. http://www.legislation.gov.uk/ukpga/2015/9/contents/enacted.
7. http://www.nationalcrimeagency.gov.uk/news/193-nca-launch-article.
8. Serious Fraud Office (2017) https://www.sfo.gov.uk/about-us/.
9. Appendix A provides details on the in-depth statistical analysis that was conducted.
10. http://www.octf.gov.uk/OCTF/media/OCTF/images/publications/NCA-Annual-Report-1314.pdf?ext=.pdf.
11. The anonymised extract excluded 416 OCGs (and 6203 nominals) flagged as 'not for dissemination' by reporting organisations and those groups originating from Police Scotland. However, it is possible that Scottish OCGs not investigated by Police Scotland appeared in the extract provided for this analysis.
12. The most common types of economic crime reported to the OCGM were: 'non-fiscal (tax) fraud' ($n = 422$); 'public sector fraud, business tax fraud/evasion (including MTIC fraud)' ($n = 218$); 'public sector fraud, personal tax fraud/evasion (including income tax/self-assessment fraud)' ($n = 213$); 'banking and credit fraud, mortgage fraud' ($n = 199$); 'public sector fraud, excise/customs duty fraud (including tobacco/alcohol fraud, fuel/oil fraud, illegal gambling)' ($n = 189$); 'identity theft'($n = 184$); 'public sector fraud, benefit fraud (non-tax credit /repayment fraud)' ($n = 166$); 'banking and credit fraud, account takeover'($n = 156$); 'insurance fraud' ($n = 150$); and 'payment card crime' ($n = 120$).
13. This included offences reported to the OCGM relating to fraudulently obtained genuine documentation—supply or use in organised immigration crime ($n = 104$), counterfeit currency (any involvement) ($n = 76$), intellectual property offences ($n = 70$) and human trafficking to exploit state benefits (age group unknown, $n = 49$), or involving adults ($n = 41$) and juveniles ($n = 13$).

References

Action Fraud. (2017). What Is Fraud and Cyber Crime? *Action Fraud* [Online]. Available at: http://www.actionfraud.police.uk/what-is-fraud. Accessed 10 May 2017.

Albanese, J. (2005). Fraud: The Characteristic Crime of the 21st Century. *Trends in Organized Crime, 8*(4), 6–14.

Button, M. (2011). Fraud Investigation and the 'Flawed Architecture' of Counter Fraud Entities in the United Kingdom. *International Journal of Law, Crime and Justice, 39*, 249–265.

Button, M., Blackbourn, D., & Tunley, M. (2015). 'The Not So Thin Blue Line After All?' Investigative Resources Dedicated to Fighting Fraud/Economic Crime in the United Kingdom. *Policing*, *9*(2), 129–142.

Button, M., Johnston, L., Frimpong, K., & Smith, G. (2007). New Directions in Policing Fraud: The Emergence of the Counter Fraud Specialist in the United Kingdom. *International Journal of the Sociology of Law*, *35*, 192–208.

Button, M., Shepherd, D., Blackbourn, D., & Tunley, M. (2016). Annual Fraud Indicator 2016. *Experian, PKF Littlejohn and the University of Portsmouth's Centre for Counter Fraud Studies*. Available at: http://www.port.ac.uk/media/contacts-and-departments/icjs/ccfs/Annual-Fraud-Indicator-2016.pdf

Cifas. (2016). *Fraudscape 2016*. London: Cifas.

City of London Police. (2015). *National Policing Fraud Strategy*. Draft Prepared by the National Police Coordinator for Economic Crime January 2015. London: City of London Police. Available at: http://democracy.cityoflondon.gov.uk/documents/s50106/Pol_24-15_Appendix_1_Draft%20Police%20Fraud%20Strategy%20v%202.2.pdf. Accessed 12 May 2017.

Cohen, A. K. (1977). The Concept of Criminal Organisation. *British Journal of Criminology*, *17*(2), 97–111.

Conseil de l'Europa (Council of Europe). (1997). *Comité d'experts sur les aspects de droit penal et las aspects criminologiques de la criminalité (PC-CO), Questionnaire*. Strasbourg Conseil de l'Europa.

Doig, A., & Levi, M. (2013). A Case of Arrested Development? Delivering the UK National Fraud Strategy Within Competing Policing Policy Priorities. *Public Money & Management*, *33*(2), 145–152.

Edwards, A. (2004). Understanding Organised Crime. *Criminal Justice Matters*, *55*(1), 30–31.

Edwards, A., & Levi, M. (2008). Researching the Organization of Serious Crimes. *Criminology and Criminal Justice*, *8*(4), 363–388.

Finckenauer, J. O. (2005). Problems of Definition: What Is Organized Crime? *Trends in Organized Crime*, *8*, 63–83.

Francis, B., Humphreys, L., Kirby, S., & Soothill, K. (2013). *Understanding Criminal Careers in Organised Crime* (Research Report 74). London: Home Office.

Fraud Advisory Panel. (2016). *The Fraud Review—Ten Years On* [Online]. Available at: https://www.fraudadvisorypanel.org/wp-content/uploads/2016/06/The-Fraud-Review-Ten-Years-On-WEB.pdf. Accessed 5 Apr 2017.

Gannon, R., & Doig, A. (2010). Ducking the Answer? Fraud Strategies and Police Resources. *Policing and Society*, *20*(1), 39–60.

Garner, S., Crocker, R., Skidmore, M., Webb, S., Graham, J., and Gill, M. (2016). *Reducing the Impact of Serious Organised Crime in Local Communities: Organised Fraud in Local Communities* (Briefing 1). Perpetuity Research and the Police Foundation. Available at: http://www.police-foundation.org.uk/uploads/holding/projects/org_fraud_in_local_communities_final.pdf

Gee, J., & Button, M. (2013). *The Financial Cost of Fraud Report 2013*. London/Portsmouth: BDO and Centre for Counter Fraud Studies.

Grabosky, P. (2013). Organised Crime and the Internet: Implications for National Security. *The RUSI Journal, 158*(5), 18–25.

HM Government. (2006). *Fraud Review: Final Report*. London: Home Office.

HMIC. (2015). Regional Organised Crime Units: A Review of Capability and Effectiveness. *Her Majesty's Inspectorate of Constabulary* [Online]. Available at: https://www.justiceinspectorates.gov.uk/hmic/wp-content/uploads/regional-organised-crime-units.pdf. Accessed 10 May 2017.

Hobbs, D. (1998). Going Down the Glocal: The Local Context of Organised Crime. *The Howard Journal of Criminal Justice, 37*(4), 407–422.

Hobbs, D. (2013). *Lush Life: Constructing Organized Crime in the UK*. Oxford: Oxford University Press.

Home Office. (2013). *Serious and Organised Crime Strategy*. London: Home Office.

Home Office. (2017). Home Office Counting Rules for Recorded Crime 2017. *Home Office* [Online]. Available at: https://www.gov.uk/government/uploads/system/uploads/attachment_data/file/602811/count-fraud-apr-2017.pdf. Accessed 10 May 2017.

Kleemans, E. R., & De Poot, C. J. (2008). Criminal Careers in Organized Crime and Social Opportunity Structure. *European Journal of Criminology, 5*(1), 69–98.

Lavorgna, A., Lombardo, R., & Sergi, A. (2013). Organized Crime in Three Regions: Comparing the Veneto, Liverpool, and Chicago. *Trends in Organized Crime, 16*, 265–285.

Levi, M., & Burrows, J. (2008). Measuring the Impact of Fraud in the UK: A Conceptual and Empirical Journey. *British Journal of Criminology, 48*(3), 293–318.

Levi, M. (2012). The Organization of Serious Crimes for Gain. In M. Maguire, R. Morgan, & R. Reiner (Eds.), *The Oxford Handbook of Criminology*. Oxford: Oxford University Press.

Mills, H., Skodbo, S., & Blyth, P. (2013). *Understanding Organised Crime: Estimating the Scale and the Social and Economic Costs* (Research Report 73). London: Home Office.

Morselli, C., Turcotte, M., & Tenti, V. (2011). The Mobility of Criminal Groups. *Global Crime, 12*(3), 165–188.

National Fraud Authority. (2011). *Fighting Fraud Together: The Strategic Plan to Reduce Fraud*. London: Home Office.

National Fraud Authority. (2013a). *Annual Fraud Indicator*. Available at: https://www.gov.uk/government/uploads/system/uploads/attachment_data/file/206552/nfa-annual-fraud-indicator-2013.pdf

National Fraud Authority. (2013b). *Fighting Fraud Together, Quarterly Update—April 2013*. London: Home Office.

NCA. (2013). National Crime Agency Goes Live. *NCA* [Online]. Available at: http://www.nationalcrimeagency.gov.uk/news/193-nca-launch-article. Accessed 10 May 2017.

NCA. (2014). *National Crime Agency Annual Report and Accounts 2013/14*. National Crime Agency.

ONS. (2016a). Overview of Fraud Statistics: Year Ending Mar 2016. *Office of National Statistics* [Online]. Available at: https://www.ons.gov.uk/peoplepopulationandcommunity/crimeandjustice/articles/overviewoffraudstatistics/yearendingmarch2016. Accessed 26 Apr 2017.

ONS. (2016b). Crime in England and Wales: Year Ending Sept 2016 [Online]. Available at: https://www.ons.gov.uk/peoplepopulationandcommunity/crimeandjustice. Accessed 26 Apr 2017.

Paoli, L. (2003). The Informal Economy and Organized Crime. In: J. Shapland, H. Albrecht, J. Ditton, & T. Godefroy. (Eds.), *The Informal Economy: Threat and Opportunity in the City* (pp. 133–172). Freiburg: Edition iuscrim.

Serious Fraud Office (SFO). (2017). *About Us SFO* [Online]. Available at: https://www.sfo.gov.uk/about-us/. Accessed 10 May 2017.

Sproat, P. (2009). To What Extent Is the UK's Anti-Money Laundering and Asset Recovery Regime Used Against Organised Crime? *Journal of Money Laundering Control, 12*(2), 134–150.

Sproat, P. (2012). Phoney War or Appeasement? The Policing of Organised Crime in the UK. *Trends in Organized Crime, 15*, 313–330. https://doi.org/10.1007/s12117-012-9154-4.

United Nations. (1976). *Fifth UN Congress on the Prevention of Crime and the Treatment of Offenders*. Report (A/CONF.169/15/Add.1). New York: UN Department of Economic and Social Affairs.

van Dijck, M. (2007). Discussing Definitions of Organised Crime: Word Play in Academic and Political Discourse. *HUMSEC Journal, 1*(1), 65–90.

van Koppen, M., & De Poot, C. (2013). The Truck Driver Who Bought a Café: Offenders in Their Involvement Mechanisms for Organized Crime. *European Journal of Criminology, 10*(1), 74–88.

van Koppen, M., De Poot, C., Kleemans, E., & Nieuwbeerta, P. (2010). Criminal Trajectories in Organized Crime. *British Journal of Criminology, 50*, 102–123.

von Lampe, K. (2015). *Organized Crime: Analyzing Illegal Activities, Criminal Structures, and Extra-Legal Governance*. Los Angeles: Sage Publications.

von Lampe, K. (2017). Available at: http://www.organized-crime.de/index.html. Latest update 7 February 2017. Accessed 11 Apr 2017.

Wilson, G. and Wilson, S. (2007). Can the General Fraud Offence 'Get the Law Right'?: Some Perspectives on the 'Problem' of Financial Crime. *The Journal of Criminal Law, 71*(1), 36–53.

Wright, A. (2006). *Organised Crime*. Cullompton: Willan.

CHAPTER 3

Routes into Organised Crime and Fraud

Abstract Drawing on interviews with 31 convicted fraudsters, this chapter explores the complex and multifaceted routes into organised crime and fraud. For the majority of offenders, their involvement in organised crime and fraud was the result of an intentional and conscious choice. Whilst for others, their route into organised crime and fraud was through recruitment (ranging from 'targeted' to 'serendipitous') by existing organised crime groups and therefore unintentional and often the result of a constrained choice. The chapter outlines how 'environmental opportunities' such as criminal, social, and business circles have an important role to play in facilitating organised criminality. The chapter considers the interplay between *intention* (whether it was a deliberate or constrained choice) and *facilitation* (whether existing work or social connections facilitated routes into organised crime) whilst highlighting the role of opportunism and how the exploitation of these opportunities facilitates routes into organised criminality.

Keywords Conscious choice • Constrained choice • Intent • Recruited • Routes in • Serendipitous recruitment • Targeted recruitment

Identifying the routes into organised crime and fraud is not a straightforward task. Complexities surround whether involvement is the result of a

T. May, B. Bhardwa, *Organised Crime Groups involved in Fraud*,
Crime Prevention and Security Management,
https://doi.org/10.1007/978-3-319-69401-6_3

deliberate decision made by an individual or is the outcome of a *constrained choice* whereby, for example, an individual has been targeted and coerced into playing a part in the criminal activities of an organised crime group (OCG). Further, there are considerations about whether involvement in organised crime and fraud is the product of fertile environmental opportunities (Smith 2014: 3), in which an individual's access to existing employment and business connections or established social and criminal networks facilitates their route into organised criminality (Kleemans 2013; Kleemans and van de Bunt 2008). This chapter charts a multilayered and messy map of pathways. Drawing on our interviews with 31 offenders (see Table 3.1), it untangles diverse, non-linear pathways into organised crime and fraud, and describes the interplay between *intention* (whether it was a deliberate or constrained choice) and *facilitation* (whether existing work or social connections facilitated routes in). The literature emphasises the role of opportunity, oft-cited as a reason for becoming involved in organised crime (Home Office 2011; National Fraud Authority 2011; Kleemans and van de Bunt 2008; Gill 2005; Morselli et al. 2011, Gill and Randall 2015; Button et al. 2016). It is argued that these opportunities are socially embedded in work and social relations and through routine activities (Kleemans and van de Bunt 2008). For example, within work settings or what has been termed 'convergence settings' (Felson 2006: 97–99; Levi 2008: 397), 'licit activities provide the opportunities as well as the social contacts needed for illegal activities' (Kleemans and van de Bunt 2008: 190).

In short, existing research has demonstrated that the knowledge accrued through daily work activities combined with the opportunities that accompany positions of trust and limited monitoring often facilitates involvement in organised crime. Using examples from the Dutch Organized Crime Monitor, Kleemans and De Poot (2008) showed how involvement is pre-structured through:

a) *Work ties* which provide requisite knowledge and access to networks
b) *Leisure* activities in which the 'underworld' and 'licit world' converge, providing opportunities to meet co-offenders
c) Negative *life events* such as divorce or bankruptcy in which some turn to illegal means for financial gain

When discussing the preconditions required to commit fraud, Cressey (1953) used the analogy of the Fire Triangle (the three requisite elements—fuel, heat, and oxygen) to develop the concept of the 'Fraud

Table 3.1 Interviewee and offence category

Unique ID	*Offender*	*Fraud type*[a]	*Length of sentence*
01	Tommy	Employee fraud	4 years
02	Dwayne	Mortgage fraud	6 years
03	Cyril	Investment fraud	10.5 years
04	Marlon	Investment fraud	11 years
05	Dexter	False accounting	7 years
06	George	Supplying articles for the use of fraud	3.7 years
07	Sandra	Money laundering	1.5 years
08	Barry	Investment fraud	3.4 years
09	Terry	Distribution fraud	9 years
10	Christian	Mortgage fraud	4 years
11	Carter	Investment fraud	2 years
12	Rolf	Supplying articles for the use of fraud	3.5 years
13	Max	Investment fraud	7 years
14	Reggie	Investment fraud	9 years
15	Bruce	Investment fraud	9.5 years
16	Claude	Debit and credit card fraud	8 years
17	Forest	Mortgage fraud	13 years
18	Jamie	Customs and revenue fraud	17 years
19	Errol	Mortgage fraud	3 years
20	Colin	Investment fraud	7.8 years
21	Bert	Insurance fraud	6.5 years
22	Steven	Tax fraud	10.5 years
23	Carl	Mortgage fraud	5.2 years
24	Sven	False accounting	13 years
25	Margaret	Tax fraud	4 years
26	Jeremy	Mortgage fraud	12 years
27	Richard	Investment fraud	5.9 years
28	Sam	Mortgage fraud	5 years
29	Wilber	Mortgage fraud	14 years
30	Daley	Investment fraud	7 years
31	Simon	Cash machine/ATM fraud	5 years

[a]For definitions of fraud type see Glossary

Triangle'. He suggested that motivation, opportunity, and rationalisation were the three requisite elements for committing fraud. Later variations of this schema have added a fourth element—'capability'—resulting in what Wolfe and Hermanson (2004) have termed the 'Fraud Diamond'. However, based on interviews with high-profile convicted Swiss and Austrian fraudsters, Schuchter and Levi have critiqued the concept of the Fraud Triangle, arguing that 'not every element is a mandatory precondition for white-collar crime' (2013: 11). The findings presented here provide new insights into the motivation of some to form new OCGs and for others to be willingly, unwittingly, or coercively recruited into existing groups.

This chapter introduces our 31 offender interviewees; building on a schema developed by Smith (2014), we unpick their often messy and complex routes into fraud and organised crime. Using illustrative case studies, the chapter shows how some offenders were recruited by OCGs to take part in existing criminal operations, whilst for others (the majority of interviewees) their route into economic organised crime was the outcome of a conscious choice. The chapter concludes by highlighting the difficulties with untangling *intention* and *facilitation* and instead suggests that offender routes into organised fraud are best understood as shaped by the conflation of the two.

Table 3.1 provides some basic information on our 31 interviewees.[1] The majority of our offenders committed fraud for personal financial gain; the remainder became involved for the status or as a result of coercion or through duplicity. Eleven interviewees disclosed that they had previous convictions, six of which had been previously convicted of a fraud offence. Other previous convictions included drink driving, driving whilst disqualified, violent disorder, criminal damage, contempt of court, possession of a firearm, handling stolen goods, and theft.

Routes into Fraud and Organised Crime

Smith (2014) has suggested that understanding the recruitment pathways of those involved in fraud and organised crime can improve how interventions are targeted. He identified two main recruitment pathways:

1. *Recruiter Pathway* in which existing OCGs seek to recruit new members
2. *Recruitee Pathway* in which those who are otherwise non-criminal make a conscious decision to become involved in organised crime

Our findings broadly echo the two pathways developed by Smith (2014). We suggest that individuals have either:

1. With no prior intention been recruited by an existing OCG
2. Made a conscious and intentional choice to become involved in organised crime and fraud

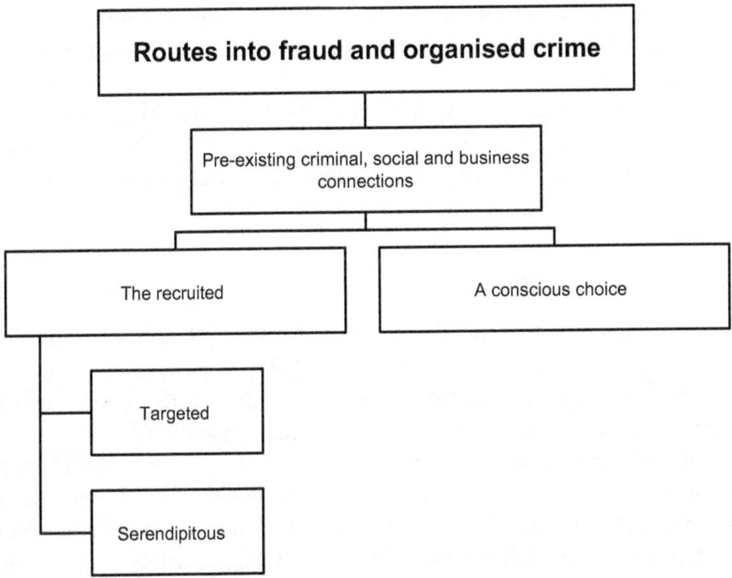

Fig. 3.1 Routes into organised crime and fraud

Our findings, however, go further to show that the routes into organised crime and fraud are facilitated by 'environmental' preconditions, for example, the existence of criminal, social, and business connections which thus adding another layer to Smith's analysis (Fig. 3.1).

A Conscious Choice

Following what Smith (2014) terms the 'recruitee pathway', the majority (24) of our interviewees had made a conscious choice to engage in fraud and organised crime. However, there were considerable differences in terms of how, when, and in what context these interviewees arrived at their decision to become involved in fraud and organised crime. For many interviewees, the decision was viewed as a means to an end—for example, the result of a failing business or messy divorce.

We have divided the criminal activity committed by this group into three categories:

1) Defrauding an employer by exploiting employment loopholes.
2) Fraud that is built into business plans and actively sought out as a way of making money.
3) Political connections were used to facilitate and hide fraud. These fraudsters committed fraud with the belief that being politically involved or having political connections would render their fraud invisible.

Defrauding a Legitimate Employer

Three interviewees (Tommy, Dexter, and Margaret) defrauded their legitimate employer. All three maintained that they had not set out to commit fraud, but all were exposed to opportunities during the course of their employment which enabled their fraud. In each case their fraud was facilitated by the absence of checks and balances and by very limited supervision of their work by their immediate managers. The National Fraud Authority has suggested that 'opportunistic frauds will occur where offenders think they can get away with it and particularly where individuals have some insider knowledge of the weaknesses of an organisation's processes' (National Fraud Authority 2011: 17). This finding is corroborated by Gill's (2005) study of 16 convicted fraudsters. The ease of committing fraud within the workplace was cited by most interviewees in his sample. Gill noted that where there is an absence of effective prevention measures coupled with an abuse of trust, 'corporate structures will continue to provide them [employees] with opportunities to generate considerable gains' (2005: 10).

Both Tommy and Dexter were convicted of fraud by abuse of position[2] and were serving seven- and four-year sentences, respectively. Tommy explained that he knew 'the system', the corporate machinery, and was able to use his 'know-how' to exploit the loopholes and siphon off funds from an account that he managed. The theme of requisite knowledge, knowing 'the system', and prior research was present in the accounts of fraud from a number of our interviewees.

Dexter, who worked for an international bank, presents somewhat of an anomaly in our sample. Unlike the other 30 interviewees, Dexter claimed that he made no financial gain from the fraud he was sentenced for[3] but was convicted for exposing his employer to unacceptable risk through false accounting.

Dexter: Organised Criminal or Risk-Taker?

At the time of arrest Dexter had been working at XX bank for a number of years. He started as an intern and gradually worked his way up to become a junior equities trader, earning £100,000 a year plus bonuses. Dexter had never been in trouble at work or with the police, and he committed many hours to working overtime, consolidating his trading knowledge and keeping abreast of the different markets. Dexter was in a job he loved and he enjoyed his working environment. The tipping point for Dexter came when his line manager left the bank and was not replaced, which left Dexter and his colleague, another junior equities trader, responsible for a multibillion-dollar trading book with no guidance or supervision. Against a volatile economic backdrop, clients began off-loading their risks onto the bank. It was Dexter's job to hedge those risks and protect the bank by using the assets in his book to offset the risk. Dexter discovered that there was an extremely fine line between, on the one hand, fraud, and on the other hand, acceptable risk-taking—an activity which Dexter maintained was encouraged and promoted at his bank.

Dexter disclosed that at his place of work junior traders were encouraged to have their own spread-trading accounts, which were set up as part of a gated community for junior traders, in essence a safe space to trade. Taking risks within this environment was actively encouraged by senior traders; the aim was to normalise risk-taking to such an extent that the skills acquired would be transferred to the junior trader's day job.

> The traders are governed by risk limits, in part ceremonial or strict, most banking organisations use risk limits ... As a manager and mentor you have to teach young, new recruits to embrace risk but they don't want to because it's scary and if you lose, you look like a tit. That's how you grow in trading. We're running a $50 billion book; we're expected to scale up our risks. You need to be pushing the boundaries; that is the mentality. When you do push boundaries, you're given a pat on the back. It's only when it goes wrong, it goes public and loss-making gets exposed.

Dexter admitted:

> I accept that my actions led to these losses but it was not criminal. My behaviour was not deemed to be dishonest in that environment.

The view of the prosecution, however, was that Dexter was 'doing it for the ego, to be the big man, to be the star trader'. Whilst he denied any criminal intent, Dexter knew that he had exposed the bank to unacceptable risk and that his actions could have had incredibly harmful consequences for the bank.

For some interviewees, whilst work provided their route into fraud, it also predetermined the type of fraud they committed. Bert, who committed cash-for-crash fraud, admitted that his place of work and his ability to successfully network provided both his route into criminality and his choice of illegal activity.

> I was originally a car valet; I ran that for 6–7 years. We would clean for solicitors, footballers, we were well contacted. I'm a networker, that's how I work. We were repairing client chips, nothing major, on-site, mobile stuff. A solicitor approached me. If you clean a car and it's been involved in an accident, I will give you £100. That's where the idea came from. I was young. I approached a solicitor in [XX City] to top the £100 that had already been offered. (Bert)

In a similar vein to Bert, Margaret's workplace also both provided the route into and specified the type of fraud committed. Margaret's case study below also illustrates the ease with which some interviewees were able to defraud large organisations when intent was coupled with an absence of checks and balances, a lack of scrutiny or auditing, and a unique understanding of their company's operating systems.

Margaret: Manipulating Loopholes

> There was no monitoring. We weren't the only ones doing it, at the time, a lot of people were doing it.

Margaret was convicted alongside her business partner Phil of defrauding a public sector organisation and falsifying tax and National

Insurance payments to the value of £1 million. They committed their fraud over a six-year period.

Margaret and Phil provided a specialist service to a public sector body whereby clients were referred to them and they were paid for the number of hours worked with clients. At first, the organisation set the number of hours to be supplied by Margaret and Phil; however, the payments claimed by Margaret and Phil should have reduced as each client's needs reduced. The fraud was simple. Margaret and Phil failed to notify their employer when the hours they worked with clients reduced and hence continued to be paid for many hundreds of hours for which they had no client contact. According to Margaret the system which allocated the work and processed the claims was flawed. Phil submitted all their invoices, adding additional hours to each invoice which were claimed as 'on call' hours.

> The public sector organisation saw this as fraudulent because we weren't physically working next to the person [client]. They provided no contract or explanation of how to claim or what you're entitled to. They saw that as unethical and started an investigation.

The fraud eventually came to light, not through scrutiny or auditing but as a result of an argument between Phil and one of the clients. The client had discovered what Margaret and Phil were doing and started to blackmail them. Phil paid the blackmailer to ensure her silence; however, she demanded more money, which Phil refused to pay. It was at this point that the blackmailer reported Margaret and Phil. In hindsight, Margaret said it was their lifestyle that gave them away:

> The lifestyle was a give-away. Turning up to work with new cars, clothes, holidays to Egypt, Mexico and my girls aged 13 and 17 are coming with me. People get jealous. I had mentioned it to Phil, I told him that clients were asking whether we were submitting proper invoices? He said, if they have any questions tell them to come and talk to me. He said, don't worry about it so I didn't, I trusted him. He said it's no problem, everything is fine. I'm doing all the invoicing; you've got nothing to worry about'. I didn't dip out of it though, the lifestyle was too good. Greed; it's a strong emotion.

Margaret was clear that the fraud she committed had been easy to do; there were loopholes. 'We didn't get into it and think we could cream this, we worked long hours. Technically, we didn't work for them; we were on call.' She maintained that at any one time they had about 40 clients, all of whom said that 'we were doing a fantastic job.'

Fraud Built into a Business Plan

For over half (18) of our interviewees, building fraud into their business plan or model as a way of making money was their route into fraud and organised crime. For some, their companies started as legitimate businesses but became illegitimate because of financial pressures or greed. Others, who positioned themselves as self-employed, had set up their own companies and appointed themselves as the company director; in doing so, their illegitimate businesses were given a veneer of legitimacy and they had the autonomy and control to undertake illegitimate business transactions. One interviewee, Terry, purposively decided to commit distribution fraud; his decision was driven by both the challenge of outwitting enforcement and the potential monetary gain. Defrauding national and multinational companies *was* his business plan, as illustrated below.

Terry: Distribution Fraud

> It's all planning, research, attention to detail and leaving no stone unturned. I'm highly organised and I never leave a trace; no prints, no DNA, nothing.

Terry was a 49-year-old man who at the time of interview was serving a prison sentence of nine years for conspiracy to defraud, money laundering, concealing criminal property, and contempt of court—after passing sentence Terry told the judge 'you've lost the fucking plot, rapists get fewer years.'

Terry left school at 16 with a handful of qualifications and a considerable desire to succeed. His pathway into fraud was in part due to choice and in part due to the circles he grew up in. Terry had lived in the same area all his life and knew a number of 'old-time fraudsters'; their motto was:

If you order three [stolen goods to fence], order 40, if you order 40 you might as well order 500. Terry believed he had been taught by the best.

> Back in the day cars were what we traded in because they were easy. I started off with bent cheques, I'd buy a cheque book, then buy 40 washing machines, I'd pay by cheque, take delivery and then sell them through my different networks. I had a buyer for electrical, a buyer for laptops, a buyer for cigarettes, a buyer for cars, alcohol, any commodity. There was no face-to-face stuff; we would sell it before we had it. I never did the meets or collected the money, I am meticulous with detail.

Eventually Terry started to tire of the monotony and the meagre rewards and decided, along with a new acquaintance, that they needed to find the perfect scam: 'we needed a formula for big money, we needed to find a scam'. Terry constantly looked for the next challenge, bored by his own success he strived to find new frauds to commit.

Finding the 'perfect' scam

Terry's perfect scam involved setting up a dummy business that masqueraded as a bona fide existing, legitimate multinational company, with the aim of stealing from other multinational companies. Terry set about creating the perfect façade for his doppelganger company. He researched the legitimate company at Companies House; he made sure that he acquainted himself with the financial, technical, purchasing, selling, and personnel structures of the company; his research was in depth and thorough. The legitimate company's logo and letterhead were copied, an almost identical phone number was purchased, and an almost identical email address set up. He cloned the company phone number which was then linked to a pay-as-you-go mobile. Terry described his scam as follows:

> *It really was the perfect scam, I'd order the goods, the stuff would make its way* [to the warehouse] *it would be delivered, picked up and sold. I'd receive the money ... all this without being seen .... I had trackers following the haulage company to ensure no police were following; I was never attached to the goods.*

Terry described how some of the people he worked alongside had no idea they were involved in anything illegal. Others were aware, but few knew about all aspects of Terry's business. Terry stole and defrauded from companies such as John Lewis, Dell, and Samsung.

Terry exercised extreme caution and was never part of the drop-off or pickup team or one of the drivers who tracked the goods from the departure to the arrival point. Terry justified his criminal behaviour by believing there were no victims: defrauding multinational companies was, in his eyes, very different to stealing or defrauding vulnerable victims: 'I wouldn't do that to an old person that's not my game.'

Describing why he committed this particular type of fraud he stated:

> *It was one of a kind. There were no real victims, for me the chase is better than the kill, will we get it, won't we, are they on to us? It really was the perfect scam.*

The demise of the 'perfect' fraud

Terry employed two young men as part of his team, one of whom was a relative. Unbeknown to Terry both were committing 'old style cheque book fraud and selling drugs'. During a night out, one of the young men was arrested for assault and released on bail. He fled the country but returned some time later and was re-arrested. As part of the assault investigation the police questioned the young man about the cheque book fraud. The young man's mother, fearful for her son and not knowing which fraud he was being questioned about, decided to 'spill the beans' on Terry's operation.

During Terry's police interviews he maintained his silence and refused to answer any police questions; he was charged with a number of fraud offences. Terry pleaded not guilty at each court hearing until the day of the trial, when he changed his plea to guilty. This decision to plead guilty had little to do with the evidence against him; his motivation to plead guilty was to keep others out of prison. Terry was, however, completely unprepared for the sentence he was given. Terry didn't regret what he had done and stated that nothing would have deterred him from becoming involved in his fraudulent activity, he maintained: *I wasn't planning on giving it up, it was too easy....*

> *If you're going to go into crime, do it to the best of your ability. Nothing would have deterred me – it was easy, lucrative and fool-proof.*

A number of offenders within the 'business plan' category refused to accept they had committed fraud; instead they described their actions as exploiting loopholes and/or merely trading within the grey area between legitimate and illegitimate practice rather than acting with criminal intent; all, however, engaged in such activity for substantial financial gain, as illustrated by the following comments from Jamie and Carl:

> It was my business. I didn't consider it as fraud. The only misdemeanour was having a grey company, but that was a loophole rather than illegal. (Jamie)

> It was my business, it was easy. I was just bending the rules. I was doing what everyone else was doing, I was just better at it. (Carl)

Conscious Choice Driven by Greed

The opportunity to make 'quick money' was, for many interviewees, a powerful motivator. Those who discussed the influence of greed tended to offset their culpability in a number of ways. Carter believed that if he hadn't conducted his fraud then someone else would have done, as highlighted below:

> Quite a lot of money was defrauded – £40,000 … I justified the crime to myself, if I didn't do it, my manager would. I knew what he was doing was dodgy. (Carter)

Steven, who was convicted of value-added tax (VAT) fraud, deliberately sought to evade paying tax at a higher rate due to his greed; his ability to do this was facilitated by his work, which was working in the film industry. Steven and his new business partners decided to put together a business proposal which was reliant on investor funding. With the business proposal accepted, certified, and 25% of the budget backed by the UK government, Steven as the organiser started to claim tax rebates in advance of the proposed work being completed. He, along with his four co-defendants, never completed any work and he was accused of misleading his backers. The prosecution's suggestion was that Steven never intended to complete the proposed work but instead sought to steal £790,000 of a potential £2.5 million from investors.

Political Connections to Facilitate Fraud

Marlon and Reggie were serving sentences for their involvement in investment fraud and Forest for his involvement in mortgage fraud, embezzlement of public funds, and money laundering. In all three cases, the interviewees were either politically involved (e.g. held political posts) or had political connections which provided a route into fraud and organised crime, perhaps suggesting that they believed their connections would offer them a layer of protection in which their involvement in criminality would be largely masked and undetected.

Forest's political connections were very much entwined with his fraudulent activity. He was convicted of mortgage fraud which dated back to 1998; in addition he was using his position as an (elected) influential political figure (outside the UK) to steal and embezzle public funds from abroad. Whilst charges were dropped and the case was dismissed in his home country, he was charged with money laundering in the UK. It was alleged that up to £50 million had been laundered through the UK, passing through around a dozen registered companies, all of which had been established to conceal his fraudulent activity. Although Forest stated that his route into crime was largely enabled by the political post he held, he pleaded guilty to the charges in court, arguing that he had made the money legitimately through his role as a consultant to a previous government in his home country before taking public office and it was this money that was used to fund his political campaigns not that of the donations to his party. He stated that it was *not unusual for public officers to be arrested and tried in his home country.*

The Recruited

Of our sample of offenders, seven (Sandra, Carter, Max, Richard, Jeremy, Errol, and Sam) were recruited by existing OCGs to become involved in fraud and organised crime. Broadly speaking, this group of offenders followed the 'Recruiter Pathway' described by Smith (2014). Their route into organised crime and fraud could be described as unintentional and unwitting. Some were recruited by strangers, others by friends, acquaintances, or work colleagues. Recruitment took on various forms; borrowing terminology from Smith (2014), it ranged from 'targeted' to 'serendipitous'.

Targeted Recruitment

Of the seven 'recruited' offenders, four (Sandra, Errol, Sam, and Jeremy) were targeted by organised criminals and recruited to fulfil a specific function within their OCG operation. Once recruited, their level of awareness regarding their involvement in an OCG ranged from willingly complicit and active to unknowing and duped. Three of them (Errol, Sam, and Jeremy) were purposefully targeted and recruited as professional enablers. They claimed to be unaware at the point of recruitment that they were being recruited to facilitate the criminality of others, who were intent on defrauding banks and mortgage lenders. Kleemans and De Poot (2008) have noted that many who become involved in organised crime are recruited because of their specialist, technical knowledge about a specific field, and this was the case for these three professional enablers.

Professional enablers are invaluable to organised criminals; they open doors that would otherwise be closed to such groups to facilitate criminal activity. Solicitors, accountants, financial advisers, bank managers, and mortgage brokers have all assisted the criminal activity of our interviewees, in addition to bank clerks, staff at retail outlets, postal workers, firemen, doormen, and casino staff. It would appear that very few professions are untouched by organised criminality, especially economic criminality.

Among our interviewees were four out of the six members of one OCG. Three of these interviewees were professional enablers; the fourth, Wilbur, was considered the linchpin of the group. The following case study illustrates how Wilber had approached recruiting two of the three professional enablers, who spoke of having had markedly different levels of involvement in the OCG.

Wilber's Process of Recruiting Enablers

Wilber was a successful professional, employed by a global company in an occupation unrelated to his fraudulent activity. By his own admission he was a risk-taker who enjoyed flirting with chance, gambling at casinos, and unpredictable ventures. He became interested in property investment in 1992, and by 2004, he had a portfolio of properties worth around £30 million, none of which, he claimed, had been bought illegally. Between 2004 and 2008 he started to conduct a small number of transactions which he considered to be bending the rules, but was in fact illegal. Below his solicitor, Jeremy, describes how he was recruited by Wilbur.

The Recruitment of Jeremy

I was a very successful conveyancing solicitor, in a small but busy practice; I had become a partner at a very young age and had no trouble bringing in work. I was introduced to Wilber as he was a successful property developer, he was very charismatic, we became friends, and I enjoyed acting on his behalf. He was fun to be with and he was worth millions. He had a gift of drawing people in, including the big companies and the letting firms. I did all his legal work; it was a delight to be his solicitor. I was young and in my 20s; after a few years I needed to borrow some money after my first divorce to help me buy a property, he lent me that money and in hindsight that is when it all started to go wrong.

In the early 2000s I started to break the rules and act unprofessionally, I was basically supporting Wilber's deceit. I trusted him and thought I could see where he was going. I have a hopeless personality in terms of being a people pleaser. I would write letters to estate agents stating that Wilber had money held with us [solicitors] to buy property when he didn't. Sometimes I would refuse to do these things for him and he would phone me up and berate me; he was an emotional bully at times. In 2006 I was chased for the deeds on a property but hadn't had a discharge certificate (evidence that a mortgage has been paid off). I, via Wilber, was supposed to have paid the mortgage off but I hadn't as we didn't have the money to do this. I wrote to the lender to buy myself an additional 14 days. In essence I was pushing through paperwork so that Wilber could complete when mortgages hadn't been redeemed. We were gathering a large deficit that we couldn't pay back, and Wilber was beginning to default on lots of mortgages. I decided at that point that I had to continue with the deceit; it was my only way out. To do this we had to keep on purchasing property illegally in the hope that we could buy ourselves out of the deficit.

When asked if anything would have deterred him from becoming involved in the fraudulent activity he was sentenced for, he replied:

> Not becoming friends with Wilber in the first place, not getting dazzled by him. Greater scrutiny from the auditors. The Solicitors Regulatory Authority did an audit and asked to see the Wilber files, the partners only gave them partial access, they covered up the fraud.

Wilber's mortgage advisor, Sam, experienced a different recruitment process to Jeremy. Both at court and during his interview he maintained that he was completely unaware that Wilber's property and land purchases were criminal or that he was laundering money for Wilber. He also claimed that he was unaware that staff he employed were bypassing regulations to process mortgage applications on behalf of Wilber. In addition he stated that he was oblivious to the fact that Wilber's bank manager was accepting bribes to complete on mortgages and Wilber's solicitor was submitting inaccurate and misleading mortgage papers. Sam only became aware that something was amiss when he received a call from his compliance department.

Sam: The Dawning Realisation of Being Part of an OCG

I received a call from my compliance department saying that we had been struck off the list of lenders. It was the head lady who called me, telling me that I couldn't submit any more applications to three particular lenders, it's to do with a client, Wilber X and his sureties. I sent a text to Wilber asking 'What the Fuck?' He invited me to lunch. I knew he was the king of bullshit, he's quick with it, so he invited me to a glitzy place. I go and sit down and there's Jeremy. Whilst at lunch Jeremy turns round and says 'Sam, Wilber has been blackmailing me, I've done lots of things I shouldn't have done, I'm in too deep, it's gone too far, but don't worry we'll sort this out, I'm going to have to resign.' Not long after that lunch he did resign and disappeared. Wilber was basically buying buildings, applying for six mortgages but only building four flats. I wanted to help, he asked if I would get a loan for him, in my name, he said he was going to set up shop—I thought he had. I thought nothing more of it until in Oct 2010 a police officer walked into my office and said he wanted to talk to me about Wilber.

A date was arranged for me to go to the station where I could explain my side of events. On the mortgage forms the information about his employment was false, he said he had been a company director earning £300k, he was in fact an [occupation] earning £100k. But I didn't sort out the mortgage someone in my office did, who just hadn't done the correct checks and had then blamed me. In 2009 I found a stunning property and asked Wilber to repay £300k that I had lent him, he was slightly evasive but said the £300k he had invested was worth millions, so he gave me £750k back. The police asked me about this—did I know he was in financial difficulty—no—the mortgage business is a boom or bust business so I wasn't concerned. That was that for a long time.

After at least a year I was called by my solicitor and told that I was going to be charged, I really couldn't believe it, my last business dealings with Wilber had been in mid-2009. The case was that I had laundered money for him, which was untrue, and lied on a mortgage application. I lent him money (for him to invest) and got it back with interest and I had nothing to do—except introducing him to the broker—with the mortgage application.

Eventually the group were unable to purchase themselves out of their deceit, and both the debts and the police caught up with them. Wilber's analysis of each individual's culpability was:

> I have no idea how the bank manager was acquitted as he was up to his neck in it and was taking bribes off me. He knew exactly what was going on as did Jeremy. Errol and Sam shouldn't have been sentenced; they really didn't know what was happening. (Wilber)

Another interviewee, Claude, was skilled at recruiting professionals; his entire business model was reliant on enablers. Rather than following Wilber's route of charm and deceit, Claude preferred to blackmail and bribe his enablers. Claude would weave his way into the social circle of junior bank clerks, spend a night drinking and taking cocaine with them, and then tease from them a fragment of insider information. The following day he would begin his blackmail; his aim was to take possession of the account details of bank customers. He rarely targeted managerial-level staff; he preferred to focus his attention on those he considered to be malleable and impressionable, for example, clerks and junior supervisors. Below, Claude describes his recruitment techniques.

Claude: Recruiting Through Blackmail and Bribery

All my most successful fraud was done through the telephone banking assimilation machines. I used enablers. I turned the straight ones into enablers through bribery. When I started I got my coke suppliers to tell me who the street dealers were in [XX city], I then got the

> street dealers to introduce me to their buyers, the bank workers. I would do a night of coke with them, get a bit of info from them, and then pay them for it. A day or two later I would ask them for more bank info—half would say no, some would try to give the money back, the women would cry. I'd bribe them and threaten them with exposure—I'd threaten to tell their employer what they did in their spare time and reveal some of the information they had already given me. I always got a few that sold info to me. All I needed was the 16 digit number and the expiry date. On my books I had postmen, telephone engineers, [exclusive gym] staff, I had a whole database of [certain gym] customers, reception staff in exclusive nightclubs, I had an insider at [online travel firm] who sold me credit details. I don't clone cards that often, I tend to nick them....
>
> I only worked in very expensive neighbourhoods, I would go into communal hallways every day, I'm not a burglar, I wouldn't go into someone's house. I would get the postmen to help me—some postmen were earning £1000s off us. I would be tipped off and given the post when a card arrived, if there was a smart card, I would take it [and] I would id the card through the return address, I would take all the cards out of their envelopes with surgical gloves, scan everything, and then post it on. A jiffy bag with the card reading equipment would arrive the following day. It was quite difficult to get the pin so I would end up impersonating all sorts of people. I'd call the victim and get the card numbers through various means then clone the smart card. Once I had a pin I could take anything, knowing that the banks would pay it back.

Both Wilber and Claude were unequivocal in the view that for their fraud to be successful recruiting enablers was essential. In Wilber's case, his fraud would not have been possible without a compliant bank manager and a submissive solicitor.

Sandra is another example of targeted recruitment. Sandra was convicted of laundering criminal assets as part of a highly lucrative and successful OCG. She was targeted and drawn into laundering money by a friend who asked if he could use her bank account to hold money for his legitimate business. Sandra allowed her account to be used and maintained that she had done this in good faith. However, she failed to question her friend about the provenance of the money, even when amounts of £100,000 were passing through her account. It transpired that her account was being used to launder money as part of an International Lottery scam. This particular scam involved individuals from across the globe who defrauded millions of pounds from victims. Sandra claimed that she never realised anything was wrong until she was arrested.

Serendipitous Recruitment

In contrast to those who had been targeted by OCGs for recruitment, there were those (Max, Carter, and Richard) whose recruitment was serendipitous. Once recruited, however, these interviewees made a conscious and very deliberate decision to exploit the criminal opportunities which they had been introduced to.

A number of interviewees maintained that their route into fraud and organised crime was as a result of taking up what they believed was a legitimate opportunity. The three recruited serendipitously were all convicted of their involvement in a highly successful boiler room fraud. Both Max and Carter stated that they had responded to what they believed was a legitimate job advertisement. Carter claimed that he had answered what he believed was a legitimate job advert which had been posted online by a finance company. Carter attended an interview in the UK and was offered a job, which he accepted. Following his acceptance of the job he was flown to Spain. In addition to a job, Carter's new employer also paid for all his travel and accommodation. Initially, he worked in a relatively junior role as an 'opener', offering investments to potential investors. It wasn't long, however, before he realised that:

> The company was fraudulent. We sold shares/investments to investors that were not the true value they said they were worth—penny shares—with the prospect that the price would go up as a result. Investors, however, were not getting their money back.

He added:

> You start to question how it works. You're kept in the dark. We couldn't even Google the company.

Similarly, Max also responded to what he thought was a legitimate opportunity, one that was offered to him by a friend. In addition to providing yet another illustration of the serendipitous route into organised fraud, Max along with Carter and Richard all provide an insight into the difficulty experienced by some of extracting oneself from the money, the 'buzz of the deal', and the lifestyle. All three were fully aware that their job was simply to defraud members of the public for financial gain, but all three continued. The case study of Max illustrates how powerful a motivator both greed and a desire for success can be.

Max

> I had a one-track mind. No one was going to come in and tell me any different. I was a bit of an arsehole.

Max had never been in trouble with the law prior to this conviction, but at age 40, he was serving a seven-year prison sentence for his part in what the prosecution described as a 'boiler room' fraud or 'organised crime dressed up as a genuine business'.

Max left college at 18 and started work in the financial sector in a clerical role. One night, whilst drinking in the pub a friend mentioned a job opportunity in Spain selling shares. Max hated his job, so called the number he had been given, spoke to the man, and was offered a job.

> I thought it was a job with an entrepreneurial spirit, working in the grey areas, working the loopholes; an early acorn that would build into a big company.

Max thought the job opportunity was perfect; he was adamant that he had 'never set out to do a fraud; I was not planning the bank job'. For Max the job opportunity came at the right time; it was his dream to be a stockbroker. At 26 he felt he was playing catch-up; he viewed the opportunity as a shortcut, to do it without the exams.

When Max arrived in Spain, he began working for a young man who wore a Rolex watch and drove a Lamborghini; for Max, it was everything he had dreamt of. Max was paid £100 a week for three months and given an apartment; he worked off commission thereafter and paid rent. Within three days of starting he was on the phones talking to potential investors. As a trader, Max worked through mailshots that he believed were authorised by a UK-based law firm; he said he felt reassured that a solicitors was involved, as it reinforced his belief in what he was doing. All the workers thought they were part of a legit job; there was no cold calling, and the lists were signed off by the law firm. The staff were, however, encouraged to engage in the 'hard sell' with potential investors.

> To make potential investors buy shares, we over-egged it, we made statements with no real evidence that stocks would go up. We were hyping it on the phone to clients … we were basically bullshitting.

When Max started as an investment trader there were four traders. Four years later, under Max's management, there were 75 people on the phones and a number of support staff. According to Max, the infrastructure was a success story. The company, however, remained unregulated. Max thought his employment was no different to a legitimate company.

> Unfortunately I let my ego run the business. The costs were off the wall, it was a false economy – we were paying out more than we were getting back.

Max viewed his business model as simply 'cutting corners'. His view was: 'If you stick to the rules, you'll never make money'. It came as a complete shock to Max when his offices were raided. Once Max learned that the police were onto him, he shut all the businesses down. Following a 'no comment' police interview, Max was bailed. Following his lawyer's advice, Max pleaded 'not guilty'. The first trial collapsed; the second trial lasted four months, and Max received a seven-year sentence.

The Preconditions: Overlapping Criminal, Social, and Business Circles

So far, this chapter has explored an individual's *intent* as a key to understanding routes into fraud and organised crime. However, in unpicking these pathways and in line with previous research, it has been suggested that overlapping criminal, social, and business circles or 'environmental opportunities' have an important role to play in *facilitating* organised criminality (Smith 2014; Kleemans and De Poot 2008). George, aged 23, was convicted of courier fraud alongside seven friends; he stated that he had learnt his 'trade' *from elders* in his social network as they were all committing the same fraud.

> I just wanted money. Everyone around me was minted. I saw others with flashy cars. You see everyone at it, you just want it. I am the youngest of four kids. I had to look after my mum and dad. My sister is an audiologist, brother a teacher [another brother living and working abroad] – they are all wealthy. I didn't want to sell drugs. I don't want to hurt anyone. I just need the money. I did feel bad for the victims. I know it's wrong but once the phone hangs up, the rest of it is forgotten. It's much easier to deal with if you don't see the victim. (George)

Similarly, Simon, aged 28, who was convicted for his part in a large-scale organised Automated Teller Machine (ATM) fraud stated that all his co-defendants were either family or friends, some he had grown up with in Eastern Europe and some he had met in the UK when he arrived. Simon made a conscious choice to engage in criminality, facilitated through his pre-existing and new social and familial ties.

Terry had also made a conscious decision to commit fraud; historically he had been involved in what he described as 'different networks', both legitimate and illegitimate. It was through these networks that he was able to orchestrate his distribution fraud. To be able to commit large-scale credit and debit card fraud, Claude had also exploited his social networks—contacts made through a history of drug trafficking and problematic drug use.

In offering an explanation for adult onset offending, Kleemans and De Poot (2008) have suggested that the 'social opportunity structure', defined as 'social ties providing access to profitable criminal opportunities' (2008: 71), offers a route into organised criminality. Further, there is often a convergence of legal and illegal activities; for example, economic fraud offenders rarely have an appreciable criminal record and often get involved in illegal activities due to an opportunity that arises from their day-to-day work or social networking (2008: 84).

Barry, who was serving a 40-month sentence for his part in an investment fraud, described his route into fraud and organised crime as 'financially motivated' and a 'short-term fix'. He explained that his then wife had been made redundant and he had been left to repay the mortgage, with the result that he felt under pressure to provide for his family. He saw the fraud as a desperate rather than greedy act. A few interviewees similarly stated that the deliberate decision to seek solutions through criminal means stemmed from financially draining divorce proceedings and settlements.

The importance of understanding the fertile ground that facilitates routes into fraud and organised crime is emphasised in the work of Levi (2008: 441), who suggested that knowing the 'fraud business' requires decentring the analysis of 'organized-ness' and refocusing attention on context, setting, and the precursors of offending. In short, academic research needs to loosen its preoccupation on analysing the organisation of fraud and focus its attention on mapping routes into fraud and creating a better understanding of the facilitators and enablers of fraud.

Conclusion

The routes into organised crime and fraud are diverse and complex. Following the work of Smith (2014), the chapter has mapped two broad categories of offenders:

1. Those who are recruited and unintentionally drawn in by OCGs
2. Those who made an intentional and conscious choice to become involved in criminality

The majority of our interviewees made a conscious choice to engage in organised fraud and were driven by financial gain. Some committed fraud by exploiting loopholes within legitimate occupations; others committed fraud by building it into business plans and actively seeking fraud out as a way of making money; others were either involved politically or had political connections and used these positions and networks to facilitate their route into organised economic crime. For the remainder of our interviewees, their route into fraud and organised crime was through either 'targeted' or 'serendipitous' recruitment by existing OCGs. Some interviewees were recruited into organised crime by strangers, others by friends, acquaintances, or work colleagues. Four of our offender interviewees were targeted by organised criminals and recruited to fulfil a specific function. Once recruited, their level of awareness regarding their involvement in an OCG ranged from willingly complicit and active to unknowing and duped. Three interviewees were purposefully targeted and recruited as professional enablers. Professional enablers were invaluable to their OCGs; they opened doors that would otherwise be closed to such groups to facilitate criminal activity. Solicitors, accountants, financial advisers, bank managers, and mortgage brokers all assisted the criminal activity of our interviewees, in addition to bank clerks, staff at retail outlets, postal workers, firemen, doormen, and casino staff. A number of interviewees maintained that their route into fraud and organised crime was the result of taking up what they believed was a legitimate opportunity. Once recruited, however, they made a deliberate decision to exploit the criminal opportunities to which they were introduced. All but one of our interviewees were involved in organised economic fraud for financial gain and greed—openly admitted or inferred—featured in most accounts of why they continued committing their crimes.

Further, the findings presented in this chapter illuminated the interplay between offender *intent* and *facilitation*. Overlapping criminal, social, and business connections provided the requisite conditions to facilitate offender routes into fraud and organised crime, highlighting how opportunities are exploited by entrepreneurial organised criminals to achieve criminal ends.

Notes

1. To protect the identity of our interviewees, we have provided no other demographic details.
2. An offence under section 4 of the Fraud Act 2006. See: http://www.legislation.gov.uk/ukpga/2006/35/section/4.
3. Whilst Dexter may not have stolen from his bank, whilst taking the unnecessary risks that he did, there is a high likelihood that he will have benefited through bonus payments that operate in many financial institutions.

References

Button, M., Shepherd, D., Blackbourn, D., & Tunley, M. (2016). Annual Fraud Indicator 2016. *Experian, PKF Littlejohn and the University of Portsmouth's Centre for Counter Fraud Studies*. Available at: http://www.port.ac.uk/media/contacts-and-departments/icjs/ccfs/Annual-Fraud-Indicator-2016.pdf

Cressey, D. R. (1953). *Other People's Money*. Glencoe: The Free Press.

Felson, M. (2006). *The Ecosystem for Organized Crime*. Helsinki: European Institute for Crime Prevention and Control, affiliated with the United Nations.

Gill, M. (2005). *Learning from Fraudsters*. London: Protiviti Ltd.

Gill, M., & Randall, A. (2015). *Insurance Fraudsters*. Kent: Perpetuity Research & Consultancy International (PRCI) Ltd.

Home Office. (2011). *Local to Global: Reducing the Risk from Organised Crime*. London: Home Office.

Kleemans, E. R. (2013). Organized Crime and the Visible Hand: A Theoretical Critique on the Economic Analysis of Organized Crime. *Criminology and Criminal Justice, 13*, 615.

Kleemans, E. R., & De Poot, C. J. (2008). Criminal Careers in Organized Crime and Social Opportunity Structure. *European Journal of Criminology, 5*(1), 69–98.

Kleemans, E., & van de Bunt, H. (2008). Organised Crime, Occupations and Opportunity. *Global Crime, 9*(3), 185–197.

Levi, M. (2008). Organized Fraud and Organizing Frauds: Unpacking Research on Networks and Organization. *Criminology and Criminal Justice, 8*(4), 389–419.

Morselli, C., Turcotte, M., & Tenti, V. (2011). The Mobility of Criminal Groups. *Global Crime, 12*(3), 165–188.

National Fraud Authority. (2011). *Fighting Fraud Together: The Strategic Plan to Reduce Fraud*. London: Home Office.

Schuchter, A., & Levi, M. (2013). The Fraud Triangle Revisited. *Security Journal*. Available at: http://www.palgrave-journals.com.ezproxy.lib.bbk.ac.uk/sj/journal/vaop/ncurrent/pdf/sj20131a.pdf

Smith, R. G. (2014). Responding to Organised Crime Through Intervention in Recruitment Pathways. *Trends and Issues in Crime and Criminal Justice, 473*, 1.

Wolfe, D. T., & Hermanson, D. R. (2004). The Fraud Diamond: Considering the Four Elements of Fraud. *The CPA Journal, 74*(12), 38.

CHAPTER 4

The Nature and Structure of Organised Crime Groups Involved in Fraud

Abstract This chapter looks at the way in which organised crime groups (OCGs) organise themselves and their operations. OCGs come in a range of shapes and sizes, and their nature and form has captured much academic attention. For example, there are questions about whether OCGs are best defined by their physical structure, the criminal activities they are involved in, or the social, cultural, and historical conditions that facilitate criminality. Academic opinion is further divided between 'those who see crimes as very well *organized*' and 'those who see crimes as intermittently or more regularly *networked* but not in any stable hierarchy' (Levi 2012: 598). Our research found a variety of organisational structures, including the classic, global, chaotic, and flat or horizontal structures. Organisational form is often dependent on the number involved in the group, the type of fraud engaged in, and the scale of the operation. The chapter presents a picture of how organised fraudsters operate, their modus operandi, how 'organised' they are, and the networks they are involved with.

Keywords Hierarchies • Networks • The classic structure • The global network • The chaotic lower tier • Flat or horizontal structure

This chapter looks at the way in which organised crime groups (OCGs) organise themselves and their operations. As a starting point to

T. May, B. Bhardwa, *Organised Crime Groups involved in Fraud*, Crime Prevention and Security Management, https://doi.org/10.1007/978-3-319-69401-6_4

understanding the nature of OCGs involved in fraud, we explore whether our offender interviewees deemed themselves and their criminal activities to be a success or failure. These reflections give us an insight into offender types, the roles and positions they occupied within their OCG, and where (if any) fault lines in their operations were found. Their subjective evaluation of success is followed by a closer look at how OCG operations are set up, coordinated, and managed. It is well known that 'OCGs are as varied as the markets they service and the activities they engage in' (Europol 2017: 13). OCGs come in a range of shapes and sizes, and their nature and form has captured much academic debate. For example, there are questions about whether OCGs are best defined by their physical structure, the criminal activities they are involved in, or the social, cultural, and historical conditions that facilitate criminality (Le 2012). Academic opinion is further divided between 'those who see crimes as very well *organized*' and 'those who see crimes as intermittently or more regularly *networked* but not in any stable hierarchy' (Levi 2012: 598). Drawing on interviews with offenders and law enforcement, this chapter highlights how OCGs involved in the fraud business can take on multiple organisational forms, with particular types of fraud (e.g. the boiler room fraud discussed below), following a similar organisational logic. By examining the structure of OCGs involved in fraud, rich insights are developed, insights which are invaluable to law enforcement professionals seeking to disrupt such groups.

Measuring Success … and Reflecting on Failure

Measuring success is an arbitrary and subjective endeavour; in business, as in life, it can be measured in varying ways: in-house promotions, additional responsibilities, salary increases, a sense of control over one's life, and job satisfaction.

> Very [successful]. I can assimilate information, very complex information and make it accessible. It is very complex but I can do it, I'm very good at what I do. I started as a filing clerk. By 21 I had been through every department. I know the system inside-out. Buy below market value, sell at bid price, and pocket the difference. Give the broker 10% for the deal, 90% for me. I have wives and girlfriends to sort out. (Cyril)

> Yes. I was [successful]. This is the only fraud I like. I can talk money out of people. Designer clothes don't come cheap. I won't ask my mum and dad because I provide for them; you just got to do it. It's wherever you park up and sit down. When I needed money I did it. I wasn't doing it every day. (George)

> I'm a good salesman. I have a passion for shares. For me, it wasn't even work. I was enjoying what I was doing. It was hard for others to compete. If you've got a passion for what you do, how can you not be good at it? (Max)

> Yes, I was successful, everything I touched turned to gold, I was, for a while, the golden boy. My own portfolio was worth millions, I had my own jet, helicopter and everything else. (Wilber)

> Yes, of course I'm successful. I'm not successful in life but in a different way – the way to survive. It's not stealing, it's just scamming. (Simon)

Some of our interviewees did, however, talk of having 'failed' either on account of having been caught or in terms of insufficient financial gain:

> I wouldn't be here if I was successful. I was technically successful, I got behind the systems, I had my enablers and I knew where to knock [defraud]. For example the [named] stores, we used to do them every day, the staff just didn't care. To be successful you need to mimic the spending habits of the victim – banks model fraud detection on fraudster habits. If you spend on someone's card in an uncharacteristic way it will flag up. If they shop at Primark and Selfridges so should you. (Claude)

> If you are going to engage in fraud, you should profit from it, I didn't, so I'm not successful. I was dazzled by a man and I lost everything. It was the banking crisis that brought it to a head. (Jeremy)

One interviewee, Jamie, did not regard his business practices as illegal. He did, however, accept that he had manipulated a loophole. In his mind his imprisonment was a punishment for his entrepreneurial endeavour and business acumen rather than for any criminality he was involved in. He saw himself as a very successful businessman and his conviction as the consequence of a government department's need to shield its accounting inadequacies from public view.

Hierarchies or Networks? What the Existing Research Tells Us About OCGs

OCGs have traditionally been depicted as tight-knit, hierarchical groups with well-defined membership roles and commanded by 'Mr Bigs' (Levi 2012; Home Office 2009; Dorn et al. 1992; UNODC 2002). This OCG structure has been described as the 'standard hierarchy' (UNODC 2002) and still remains the most common type of OCG structure dominating criminal markets, according to Europol (2017). However, others have suggested that OCGs in the UK are non-hierarchical, based on loose networks, composed of specialist offenders working together for the duration of criminal projects (Levi 2012; Home Office 2009). Europol has suggested that between 30% and 40% of OCGs operating at an international level are characterised by loose networks and only 20% coalesce for short-term ventures (Europol 2017). A study conducted by Francis and colleagues which examined criminal careers in organised crime examined a sample of 4112[1] offenders identified on the Police National Computer (PNC). This showed that they were involved in a variety of crime types, with only 12% specialising in particular—mainly drug-related—offences (Francis et al. 2013). To capture the diversity of criminal activities and the fluid network of participants involved, others have preferred the concept of 'crime enterprises' (van Duyne 1996) or 'enterprise crimes' (Kirby and Penna 2010).

Finckenauer argued that:

> [W]hat we more commonly see are loosely affiliated networks of criminals who coalesce around certain criminal opportunities. The structure of these groups is much more amorphous, free floating, and flatter, and thus lacking in a rigid hierarchy. (2005: 65–66)

Noting that a formalised structure is often lacking and that groups are increasingly fragmented, criminologists have suggested that organised crime is in fact 'disorganised' (Wright 2006; Reuter 1983), or at least unorganised. Drawing on empirical examples and critical of the 'structural determinism' (1998: 412) inherent in archetypical descriptions of organised crime networks, Hobbs has suggested that local OCGs are diverse, flexible, opportunistic, and contingent networks, which exist on the borderlands between licit and illicit, local and global. Described as 'hubs', Hobbs states:

> [T]hese individuals operate within multiple cross-cutting networks of criminal and legitimate opportunity: they are not 'gang members', nor have they pledged allegiance to some permanent structure, but constitute hubs of action and information linking networks featuring webs of varying densities. (1998: 412)

Similarly, Lavorgna et al. (2013) in their comparative study of organised crime in three regions (the Veneto in Northern Italy, Liverpool in the UK, and Chicago in the United States) suggested that whether defined as Mafia-type groups, gangs, or transnational OCGs, definitions are locally contingent and reflective of social and political contexts. Drawing on the work of Thrasher (1927), their findings support the argument that 'no two gangs are alike and that differences in personnel, experience, and tradition combined with the physical and social environment give every gang its own peculiar character' (Lavorgna et al. 2013: 282).

The Police Perspective

In line with the research literature, the police officers we interviewed suggested that OCGs involved in fraud took on multiple organisational structures. Police descriptions of OCG structures were closely tied to descriptions of what they viewed as the 'typical' fraudster involved in organised crime. Although police officers sometimes discussed fraud investigations that involved individuals acting alone (making up the bulk of the caseloads in two police force regions), it was estimated that 'the majority', or as much as 90%, of the fraud cases investigated were committed by OCGs. It was argued by several police officers that fraud was rarely committed by an individual acting alone. As one officer stated: 'It's very unusual for one person to be responsible without having co-conspirators' (EP14). Instead, as highlighted in previous chapters, officers were very much of the opinion that fraud investigations, more often than not, involved several individuals, often including professional enablers who purposefully assemble to commit fraud.

Q: What proportion of your case load are OCGs as opposed to lone traders?

A: The majority really. I deal mainly with the Romanian-type work but still do bank insiders working for national and high street banks – that type of crime.

Q: So they're [bank insiders] your lone traders?
A: They're not really lone traders because even though they're individuals who are accessing the systems at their bank and providing data, they can give it to a third party who is part of a conspiracy elsewhere. The group's organised in such a way they need that person from the bank. In that sense they're still attached to an organised group. (EP21)

In describing the profile of offenders involved in organised fraud, police officers described, to a greater or lesser degree, a typical economic fraudster as a 'white-collar villain'—older, from an educated or professional background and with little or no prior criminal involvement. For some police officers, this profile was associated with what they viewed as the 'classic' OCG structure, hierarchical and pyramidical in form. Within this classic structure, a fraudster tended to assume a position higher up the chain of command—'not visible and hence … getting everyone else to do the dirty work on their behalf' (EP15)—and in possession of the requisite know-how to be able to facilitate the fraud. This particular profile was found to exist amongst those involved in 'major fraud', perpetrated by 'what you'd call respectable business people or professional people' (EP9) as opposed to those committing low-level fraud 'that happens on the street, etc., you know, card skimming and things like that' (EP9).

> I would say they [organised fraudsters] were at least 40 years and over. I wouldn't say I've met any fraudsters younger than that or have come across them in any of my inquiries. Obviously the crash-for-cash inquiry I'm dealing with, the main perpetrators are older but obviously the people involved in the cars might be younger. But I would say the main perpetrators are, you know, 40s or above. (EP4)

Moving away from the classic representation of an OCG network, other police officers argued that a slightly different structure has emerged, one which is characterised by loose, slightly more dynamic networks of offenders who work together in a synchronised and complementary way to commit fraud. As this officer stated:

> I think a good percentage of the frauds we investigate are like an OCG that is a group of individuals who may align themselves, then you get the

> professional enablers and more cross-border [networks]. ... There's not so much one particular person controlling a group of individuals in a hierarchy ... But there is a degree of organisation, be it that they'll be an accountant or there'll be a solicitor or there'll be some form of professional enabler, allowing ... the operation of the fraud to take place. So a lot of our enquiries do involve a structure and a number of individuals working together to fulfil their part. (EP10)

Greater fluidity in organisational form prompted some police officers to argue that the image of a 'typical' fraudster is eroding and becoming somewhat outdated. These officers suggested that as more OCGs move into fraud or certain types of fraud, such as cash-for-crash or boiler room fraud, the profile of the group dynamic changes. This was highlighted by police interviewees who commented that they are now arresting a younger, more criminally diverse group of offenders involved in organised fraud.

> Historically it's [the typical profile of a fraudster] true but I think it's changing because of the way society's evolving, with the internet especially there's a lot more fraud now ... So, I don't accept that it's just older people any more. It's very much a changing dynamic. (EP16)

> I think, the longer I'm in fraud I think the landscape of fraud is certainly changing ... I think, whereas it would be your, perhaps your older, more mature person involved in fraud and maybe your accountant, your bank managers, I think now, there's lots of young people, certainly in the world of boiler room fraud ... you have your young teenagers enticed into working in boiler rooms and with no qualifications or work experience that are entering into the world of fraud. (EP14)

> I would say the majority of the work on the operational [side of policing] tends to be boiler room type fraud. And I would not say that any of them are older offenders with limited or no previous convictions. A proportion of them'll be early 20s, even younger. (EP15)

In addition to the perspective provided by our enforcement interviewees, our convicted offenders also provided us with further insights into the changing structure of OCG fraud, highlighting the diversity and complexity of many of the new and emerging associations.

The Classic Structure

What was seen as the classic structure—pyramidical in form—with a 'top-down' structure of governance was referred to by some of our police interviewees as noted above. Convicted for his part in a distribution fraud alongside five others, offender Terry described his position at the top of what was a classic pyramid-shaped OCG, from where he was able to coordinate the roles of the individuals beneath him who were brought in as and when required. These individuals made up the middle and lower tiers of his OCG network. Whilst Terry knew everyone he employed in his network, none of his employees knew one another. This way he ensured that his subordinates did not set up in competition and that he protected 'his' network from any concerted enforcement activity. The fewer relationships and lines of communication that existed, the less likelihood there was of the entire group being dismantled by enforcement. For Terry's operation to be a success, a 'rigid hierarchy' with a 'single boss' was deemed necessary (UNODC 2002: 19).

The Global Network

A variant of the classic structure was described by a number of interviewees who were serving custodial sentences for their involvement in boiler room fraud (Max, Carter, Richard, and Bruce). The boiler rooms were set up and run from a base in Spain; whilst classic in structure, there was an added complexity which was the global division of labour. We described this OCG structure as 'the global network'. Whilst the OCG operation in Spain was structured with a tiered, clear division of labour, other aspects of the OCG operated abroad. For example, Bruce who held a management position as part of a boiler room fraud based in Spain had offices across the globe, including a due diligence team set up in the United States that he liaised with.

Max, who held a middle management position in a Spanish boiler room, discussed having trusted associates in the UK who were responsible for producing falsified certificates and posting them to investors. The global reach of organised criminals poses difficulties for enforcement agencies seeking to disrupt their activities. The accounts of Max and Bruce, both of whom were part of the same OCG, provided an insight into the workings of a boiler room from the middle and upper tiers of the classic OCG structure. Having worked his way up the ranks, Max described himself as a middle ranking manager, overseeing the sales team beneath him and liaising with the top tier management. Following verification from his supposed due diligence team, Bruce sold investments to Max's company for Max's company to then sell onto investors. In contrast, within the global network, Carter was positioned at the bottom of the hierarchy after responding to what he thought was a legitimate job opportunity in Spain. Earning a commission-based salary, he worked as part of the sales team, calling potential investors from share lists he had obtained from management positioned in the tier above. After a few weeks of working, Carter realised that what he was doing was on the fringes of illegality, but chose to continue.

Further examples of the global network were provided by examining the criminal activities described by Marlon, Reggie, and Forest who were either politically involved (e.g. held political posts) or had political connections which they used to facilitate fraud. Marlon, Reggie, and Forest were all involved in OCG operations that relied on key contacts and global connections and that were held together by personal loyalties and ties that were seen as central to the success of the OCG's criminal activities (UNODC 2002: 14).

The Chaotic Lower Tier

Another variation of the classic structure was explained to us by Claude, who operated between the top and bottom tiers of his particular OCG structure. Claude was part of what appeared to be a hierarchical classic pyramidical OCG management structure; the tier above Claude (his bosses) appeared to operate in a classic boardroom style (Claude, however, refused to discuss the tier above him during the interview). Only Claude populated his tier and below him was a loose, transient population of individuals whose recruitment and management was fluid. Those working at this level of the organisation were best described as free-flowing contractors, who were recruited through a variety of means, one being bribery, another coercion. They tended to work as and when they were needed.

With respect to the ATM fraud in which he was involved, Simon explained that different roles and functions were divided between OCG members, with each role and position attracting different rewards.

> They [co-defendants] don't all do the same thing. Some handle the money, some go to stick the device [the card reader on the ATM machine], a different guy goes to collect, and some sleep and wake up rich.

> Not everyone made the same money, everyone got different amounts. Do you and your boss get the same pay?

Simon's account indicated the presence of a structural hierarchy below which was a more diffuse network. He explained that once OCG members had learnt the ropes, they could set up their own smaller criminal enterprises. This had been the case for him and his co-defendants. It also appeared to be the source of tension between Simon and his brother who was also serving a custodial sentence for the same offence.

> Yeah, you make money [but] in the end you still have nothing. Go in the morning, stick the device in, and collect it in the evening. You can make £200,000 – £300,000 a day in areas like Chelsea, Fulham, Marble Arch. Sometimes [you] make £10,000 a day in other areas like Whitechapel – where it is poor – Hackney, North London. It takes a few seconds to download but about 10 hours to translate. You can't do it as a daily job. You'd go on a Friday and Saturday and then 2–3 weeks you're off and you don't touch the device and you spend the money. I spent the money on cars, clothes, girls, holidays and drugs – cocaine of course! (Simon)

The Flat or Horizontal Structure

In the previous chapter we discussed a group of interviewees who had made a conscious choice to engage in organised crime and fraud and who were convicted for defrauding their employers. Interestingly, these interviewees were a part of smaller OCGs made up of two or three co-conspirators, not all of whom were convicted when the case went to trial. Their operations were dependent on their skill set, level of autonomy, and lack of supervision in their place of work and required the assistance of only one or two others. Such OCGs were flat or horizontal in organisational form, with an almost equal division of labour, despite co-defendants evading conviction.

Conclusion

The police officers we interviewed suggested that OCGs involved in fraud take on multiple organisational structures; this was reflected in our analysis. In describing the profile of offenders involved in fraud, some police described the profile of offenders as often older, from an educated and/or professional background and with little or no prior criminal involvement.

This profile was associated with what they viewed as the classic OCG structure, hierarchical and pyramidical in form. Other police officers argued that a slightly different structure had emerged, one which was characterised by loose, slightly more dynamic networks of offenders who work together in a synchronised and complementary way to commit fraud. These police officers argued that the image of the classic fraudster is eroding and becoming somewhat outdated. Another OCG structure was the global network structure; this followed a similar business model to the classic structure but operated at a European or an international level. The final derivative of the classic OCG structure was characterised by a hierarchical top tier and fluid or chaotic lower tiers. In many respects, the classic, hierarchical structure is the most dominant form of fraud-related OCGs, but in many ways this has adapted to account for the geographical spread of OCG operations across borders and for different types of organised fraud. This chapter has shown that OCGs involved in fraud are heterogeneous, rather than being *either* hierarchical structured *or* loose networks.

Note

1. One hundred and thirty-one inclusion offences, using the Home Office Code Index, were considered.

References

Dorn, N., Murji, K., & South, N. (1992). *Traffickers: Drug Markets and Law Enforcement*. London: Routledge.

Europol. (2017). EU Serious and Organised Crime Threat Assessment: Crime in the Age of Technology. *Europol* [Online]. Available at: https://www.europol.europa.eu/newsroom/news/crime-in-age-of-technology-%E2%80%93-europol%E2%80%99s-serious-and-organised-crime-threat-assessment-2017. Accessed 26 Apr 2017.

Finckenauer, J. O. (2005). Problems of Definition: What Is Organized Crime? *Trends in Organized Crime, 8*, 63–83.

Francis, B., Humphreys, L., Kirby, S., & Soothill, K. (2013). *Understanding Criminal Careers in Organised Crime* (Research Report 74). London: Home Office.

Hobbs, D. (1998). Going Down the Glocal: The Local Context of Organised Crime. *The Howard Journal of Criminal Justice, 37*(4), 407–422.

Home Office. (2009). *Extending Our Reach: A Comprehensive Approach to Tackling Organised Crime*. London: The Stationery Office.

Kirby, S., & Penna, S. (2010) Policing Mobile Criminality: Towards a Situational Crime Prevention Approach to Organised Crime. In K. Bullock, R. V. Clarke, & N. Tilley (Eds.), *Situational Prevention of Organised Crimes*. Cullompton: Willan.

Lavorgna, A., Lombardo, R., & Sergi, A. (2013). Organized Crime in Three Regions: Comparing the Veneto, Liverpool, and Chicago. *Trends in Organized Crime, 16*, 265–285.

Le, V. (2012). Organised Crime Typologies: Structure, Activities and Conditions. *International Journal of Criminology and Sociology, 1*, 121–131.

Levi, M. (2012). The Organization of Serious Crimes for Gain. In M. Maguire, R. Morgan, & R. Reiner (Eds.), *The Oxford Handbook of Criminology*. Oxford: Oxford University Press.

Reuter, P. (1983). *Disorganised Crime: Illegal Markets and the Mafia—The Economics of the Visible Hand*. Cambridge, MA: MIT Press.

Thrasher, F. M. (1927). *The Gang*. Chicago/London: University of Chicago Press.

UNODC. (2002). *Results of a Pilot Survey of Forty Selected Organized Criminal Groups in Sixteen Countries*. Global Programme Against Transnational Organized Crime. United Nations Office on Drugs and Crime.

van Duyne, P. C. (1996). *Organised Crime in Europe*. New York: Nova Science Publishers Inc.

Wright, A. (2006). *Organised Crime*. Cullompton: Willan.

CHAPTER 5

Cops and Twenty-First-Century Robbers

Abstract This chapter provides an insight into the challenges faced by enforcement agencies when investigating organised crime groups involved in fraud, including whether and how to prioritise organised crime group fraud cases, the perception that fraud is a 'victimless' crime, the length and complexity of investigations, and the difficulties of working across jurisdictions. The views of enforcement professionals are juxtaposed with those of the 31 offender interviewees. The chapter provides a sombre account of the challenges faced by asset recovery teams when tracing victims' money, money that has dispersed across bank accounts and borders within a matter of minutes. The reader is also provided with the striking comparison between the speed with which organised criminals are able to adapt their business practices and move money across jurisdictions to the world of policing, where investigations are complex, lengthy, and mainly reactive.

Keywords Asset recovery • Confiscation orders • Cultural blindness • Enforcement challenges • Prison networks • Technological challenges • Trial by jury

Over the last ten years the types of fraud committed and the demographic profile of those committing fraud have changed. Reports made to the police and Action Fraud[1] have increased significantly, and the move from

T. May, B. Bhardwa, *Organised Crime Groups involved in Fraud*,
Crime Prevention and Security Management,
https://doi.org/10.1007/978-3-319-69401-6_5

offline to online fraud has been rapid. In 2015/16 the Office for National Statistics estimated that there were 3.6 million fraud offences in the 12 months to June 2016 (ONS 2016), though the proportion that is committed by organised crime groups (OCGs) remains an unknown. Advances in technology and the relative anonymity of offenders have both contributed to and facilitated the rise in this type of criminality, which has seen new offenders entering the criminal marketplace and, with it, new policing dilemmas.

Since 2010 cuts to the UK's public purse have affected the entire public sector, presenting the 43 forces of England and Wales and specialist national enforcement agencies with a number of challenges; there have been reductions in police officer and staff numbers, cuts in spending on goods and services, and in many forces a realignment of how the craft of policing is applied to everyday demands. Against this backdrop, investigating cases of fraud and bringing prosecutions to a successful conclusion pose a number of hurdles for enforcement agencies, including whether and how to prioritise OCG fraud cases, the complexity of cases and of working across jurisdictions, a lack of resources and specialist officers, the length of investigations, the perception that fraud is a 'victimless crime', and the inherent difficulties of partnership work. In 2008 Harfield identified several prerequisites for effective policing of organised crime, including the need for:

- Appropriate legislation
- Instruments enabling cooperation and collaboration
- Investigator collaborative structures
- Agencies with appropriate powers
- Preventative effort
- Knowledge management and information sharing

Almost a decade later economic crime investigators continue to cite Harfield's prerequisites for policing organised crime, in pointing to the most pressing challenges facing enforcement professionals and civilian investigators today.

In this chapter we examine the policing and sentencing of organised fraud, mainly from the perspective of policing professionals. We start by examining the decision-making processes behind whether to investigate a case or not and from that the parameters of investigations; we move on to discuss some of the difficulties faced by policing professionals, looking specifically at the complexity of investigations, resource allocation, and the cultural challenges identified by policing professionals which hamper economic crime investigations. In the second half of the chapter we present the views of enforcement professionals and offenders regarding the Crown Prosecution Service (CPS) and the court process, presenting data on the number of interviewees subject to court orders, such as Serious Crime Prevention Orders (SCPOs) and Financial Reporting Orders (FROs),[2] both of which aimed to curb an offender's ability to commit further economic criminality. Finally, we conclude the chapter by presenting a snapshot view from our offenders of the ability of the prison service to disrupt associations and networks.

The Allocation of Cases and Setting the Parameters of an Investigation

Investigations involving OCGs involved in fraud tend to be complex and can take many months or years to reach a conclusion. Conducting a successful investigation requires a thorough knowledge of both the investigative process and the legislation. As discussed in Chap. 2, all fraud reports either at the point of reporting or at the investigative stage should be documented or processed by Action Fraud. Several officers discussed the problems associated with such a system, and many viewed the central reporting function of Action Fraud as problematic; however, as flawed as most thought the current system is, no officer was able to suggest a better alternative. Officers all agreed that monitoring fraud reports is an important element of tracking trends and gathering intelligence on possible organised groups involved in fraudulent activity, as described by the officer below:

> I can see the idea [of Action Fraud] is a good idea. If you get 50 people reporting a similar type of crime from the same email address then pulling that together is good, otherwise you're going to get one police officer who will investigate it in one place, one in another and one in another. However, it can leave victims feeling like we're [police] a faceless organisation. You've [victim] lost money and you just get a letter saying, 'This will not be investigated.' If, on the other hand, they see that Mr. Police Officer has turned up, taken a bit of care and interest and empathised with them, and said, "Sorry, it doesn't look like we've got any lines of enquiry," that's a better approach. I had to deal with somebody who had £25,000 stolen out of his

> bank account. Somebody had cloned his card and withdrawn £25,000. The bank refunded him the money but he reported it to the police. It was sent to Action Fraud, they looked at it and sent a letter back saying, 'As the bank has refunded you the money, we've not got a complainant so we're not going to investigate it.' Because the banks aren't willing to make a complaint, the system doesn't seem to work. (EP4)

At a local level, priority setting appeared to be fluid; regional and local teams tended to examine the merits of each case to then decide whether or not to investigate. One commonality across our enforcement interviews, when deciding on whether or not to investigate a case, was the vulnerability of a victim, which was always reported as a key consideration in decision-making. A victim was considered vulnerable if they were elderly or young, had a learning difficulty, mental health issue, and/or emotional vulnerabilities. If any of these criteria were met, a preliminary investigation was nearly always initiated. A number of other factors were highlighted by officers as relevant to the decision to investigate. These included the value of the fraud; if bribery or corruption of a public official was involved; if the fraud was cross border; and if it was linked to a government, regional, or local priority. Another important criterion is if fraud or money laundering is linked to serious criminal activity, for example, firearms offences, terrorism, people trafficking, or other serious organised criminality.

Whilst discussing the complexity of cases, officers spoke about the importance of containing and focusing investigations. It was suggested that deciding on an investigation's parameters as soon as practicable often created the best possible chance of achieving a successful result for victims. Unwieldy investigations which attempt to cover all aspects of a case and take statements from every victim were viewed as unworkable and problematic, as the following quotes illustrate:

> The volume of the material. The number of people bailed – if you've got 20 people bailed and you've got to get all of those cases developing, gathering the evidence, getting the bank statements, the forensic examinations, trying to show the associations, the associations between them. You get past one challenge and you're straight into the next one. It's spinning plates. We all have that but I think fraud cases are particularly difficult. I mean, if you've got a burglary, it's one statement, plus you've got multiple victims with fraud, maybe as many as 300. And you've got to adhere to the Victims' Charter and do regular victim updates. If you do it right it works really well. I had all mine on an email contact list and I would send them emails and the

> feedback I got from the updates was really, really good. And I think I agreed a 10% statement so of the 300 I only took 30 statements as evidence for the trial. But it's about managing that with the sheer amount of people involved. (EP18)

> There's no quick jobs in this area of work, people don't understand, particularly the public; they don't understand what's involved, how long it takes to even do a 'simple quick job' in inverted commas, it can take you three to six months and that's quick. Simply because of the time it takes to go to court to get the production orders to investigate the account. You have to wait for the initial product to come back, the bank statements, then you have to have a look at them and decide which transactions are relevant. You then have to send off for the subsequent request then wait, at least another three or four weeks to get that back .... With financial investigations you just don't know where it's going to lead you, so it's impossible to say at the beginning how big is it going to be. One job, that was supposed to be a quick hit, as our then sergeant liked to call it, turned into 18 months and £11m and seven defendants. You just don't know what you're going to find. (EP30)

Many officers discussed how their successful prosecutions rarely involved investigating each and every element of a case or taking statements from each and every victim; many of the offences our offender interviewees had been convicted of involved multiple victims, in some cases running into thousands (of victims). Officers highlighted that, besides a conviction, a successful case is often about curtailing the criminality of those who are suspected of causing the greatest harm and targeting those who harbour realisable assets; one consequence of such an approach is that professional enablers often remain untouched. Police interviewees often spoke of their frustration at the lack of enforcement activity directed at professional enablers. Whilst professional enablers can be integral to OCG activity, in many investigations they remain untouched. Remaining outside the remit of an investigation is not, however, a reflection of policing priorities or a lack of interest from enforcement professionals but is often one of the casualties of contracting enforcement budgets and the need to focus an investigation on recovering an offender's assets and stopping the primary criminality and its associated harm at source. Enforcement interviewees were unequivocal and unanimous in their view that if the resources—both time and money—were available, investigations against enablers would undoubtedly become as important to the investigation as the other members of an OCG tend to be. Many of our offender interviewees were aware of the constraints police officers face when investigating fraud and the hurdles they need to clear before they are able to mount an investigation, leaving many of our offenders believing that they were both untouchable and uncatchable.

The Challenges Faced by Enforcement Agencies

The challenges to policing fraud are well cited in the academic literature. Historically, fraud has been viewed as a low-policing priority and often met with a lack of interest (Doig et al. 2001; HM Government 2006; Fraud Advisory Panel 2016; Button et al. 2007; Button 2011; Button and Tunley 2015; Levi and Burrows 2008; Doig and Levi 2013). In outlining the challenges confronting the delivery of the National Fraud Strategy, previous research by Doig and Levi (2013) found that efforts have been thwarted by an over-emphasis on 'front-line policing', diminished police resources for fraud investigations with the elimination of (local) police fraud squads, continued financial constraints, and the competing policing priorities of counter-terrorism, organised crime, and implementing the Proceeds of Crime Act (PoCA) 2002.

Understanding and investigating organised criminals involved in fraud is challenging. The complexity of investigations (in particular cross-border/jurisdiction cases), the threat posed by new technologies, resource issues, and the difficulty of initiating fraud investigations were all issues highlighted by our enforcement interviewees as everyday difficulties they experience as specialist investigators.

The Length and Complexity of Fraud Investigations

The ease and relative invisibility with which organised fraudsters are able to commit fraud was a recurring theme to emerge from our offender interviews; this was, however, in stark contrast to our enforcement professionals who described fraud cases as time consuming, frustrating, and complex. It appeared that the simpler the fraud was to commit, the more complex the investigation. As more than one officer commented, investigating fraud and chasing a victim's money was akin to 'chasing ghosts'. Once an investigation has been initiated, however, the complexity of the case and the length of time taken from inception to completion tended to pose serious challenges to investigators. It was not unusual for interviewees to discuss cases which took longer than three years to complete, particularly when enquiries involved European or international investigative work. Cross-border work was viewed as particularly problematic for UK-based officers.

> When you're making enquiries overseas if you send a request off, a letter of request, it's going to be 12 months before you get a response and then you've got to assimilate the evidence and translate it, all at a huge cost. (EP6)

> The time it takes to do things is a challenge. You're getting documents from banks, which, unless you have a court order they can only do what they can do. The systems they have for recording things and recovering things, it takes time. The time it takes to analyse information. I mean, we go out and do a search and you recover 10 bags of documents. That's a mammoth, mammoth amount of work for one person. (EP12)

Complexity at a European Level

The geographical spread of organised crime beyond national boundaries—the 'new menace' of transnational organised crimes (Finckenauer 2005)—demands a seamless cross-border policing response and an expansive policing infrastructure that extends beyond the capacity and capabilities of the police (Home Office 2012; Harfield 2008). However, negotiating different national laws and judicial systems in a transnational context can be both costly and time consuming with the result that the mobility of transnational OCGs is rarely met with a commensurate mobile response from the police and other law enforcement agencies (Penna and Kirby 2013).

Cross-border policing is a challenge to both the capacity and capabilities of traditional policing. On a practical level, there is often a language barrier coupled with the issue of incompatible legislation; extradition can be problematic, and signing working agreements takes considerable patience and involves the cooperation of the CPS and the equivalent organisation in the overseas jurisdiction. In addition, cross-border work is extremely costly and the investigative process is often slow. The case study below illustrates the difficulties of working across Europe and how these difficulties can be overcome to conclude in a successful prosecution.

Boiler Room Fraud: Working in Partnership Across Europe

The one thing we didn't appreciate was Spain hasn't got a Fraud Act.

This is why over the years we've had issues getting stuff out of Spain, they haven't got like-for-like legislation. It's not seen as being as important to them. There, fraud is a magistrates' court issue and serious and organised crime is an upper court one. Only when you get to the upper court do we get all the toys and technical stuff to use.

On this particular case our strategy was to target the top enablers; so we go to Spain and contact the Spanish team who've agreed—reluctantly—to work with us, so we sorted out an agreement and signed it. We've got an operations team in [UK city] and one in [Spanish city], both working on the same targets, myself as Senior Investigating Officer (SIO). My investigating officer went out there every month for six months. We wondered what we were doing there 'cos neither of us spoke Spanish so we had an Ethiopian woman translating for us, she was our sole means of communication with the Spanish team. There were times when clearly things weren't going well and we'd said something that we shouldn't have done—their hands went up in the air and they were getting all Mediterranean with us. It was difficult but over time we got to know each other. Every Friday, regardless of how busy we were, we'd phone up and talk.

We started to build the victim statements, telling the Spanish team who we were interested in, what frauds, and which victims, and they did all the banking stuff. The idea was to build a file together that we could present to the Lower Court, if they adopted it, we'd be at a starting point. Achieving that took us nine months. After nine months they decided to go to court to get intercepts to help us get evidence to use in court. The court set us tasks; we had to prove it was organised crime for us to then be able to go to a judge, which took another six months. We weren't just looking at one person but the top 15.

When our targets flew into meet, we'd use mobile surveillance and listening devices. We eventually built up the case and got an appointment to meet one of the five Supreme Court judges in Spain. At that point we agreed who was going to prosecute who and what jurisdiction was going to do what. The judge said yes and asked the Spanish team what they needed to get it to court. Within a month the Spanish had put 51 people on intercept, it was like a spider's web, with our targets in the middle. Every criminal phone call they made or received relating to criminal activity, the other person then went on our list. Suddenly we had lights going out all across [a city], we picked up everything from firearms to drugs.

The judge signed a 90 -day warrant for the intercepts and that was our countdown to arrest. Forty of our officers went out for the operation, joining about 300 Spanish officers; in total we arrested 121 people. Because the boiler rooms don't open 'til later in the day the idea was to pick people off one by one, keep it quiet, so they'd get more people turning up to work, more business for us. The first guy walked out of his house in his pyjamas to take his rubbish out, Spanish officers jumped over his fence, hauled him off, and threw him in the back of the van. Five minutes later his wife was standing at the window wondering where he'd gone. She phones him and another officer dressed up as a postman knocks at the door and arrests her. The court remanded 20 people, the other 90 are on bail; we had about 30 people on bail in the UK. Four cases have gone through court already, ending up in sentences—some got five years, others seven, the main ones are still to come back; there's five or six we're ready to extradite now. The public is aware of it [boiler room fraud] now. Our victims lost everything, for older people, even the middle-aged, they're never going to get the chance to recover financially from this fraud—it's life-changing.

Q: Are you going to be able to seize any assets?
A: Yes, but it'll never be enough. I will be shocked if it's 10% of the value.

Whilst working across jurisdictions is a complex, costly, and lengthy process for enforcement personnel, offenders appear to work and manage their businesses across the globe with relative ease. One of our offender interviewees who sold shares to 'brokers' (boiler room operatives) across the world described how he worked with both licensed and unlicensed brokers from 'Spain, Holland, Sweden, Asia, Taiwan, Hong Kong, New

Zealand; all over the place' (Bruce). The comparison is stark between the ease with which offenders cross borders and legal jurisdictions, and the logistical difficulties experienced and legal requirements which must be met before enforcement professionals are able to mount a cross-border investigation.

Technological Challenges

The gap between the technology available to organised criminals and to police officers was incalculable. Organised fraudsters have the necessary technology at their fingertips and are able to purchase the professional expertise to apply the latest technology to their businesses. Whilst police budgets have been cut by millions in the last seven years, the profits of organised criminals seem to have increased at the same pace, if not faster. Put simply, raising revenue for organised criminals is unproblematic, but highly problematic for the police. Officers frequently highlighted the problems enforcement has in keeping up with organised fraudsters; it appears that they no longer play cyber leap-frog with OCGs but a frustrating and demoralising game of hide and seek, in which the police are constantly but ineffectually doing the seeking. The speed with which organised criminals are able to adapt their business practices and their superior technological resources and capacity leave the police with very little choice but to react to criminal activity for the most part, rather than proactively try to prevent it:

> Imagine how easy fraud actually is, and if you can get cyber enabled you can be very remote from the crime scene. Our investigative techniques, it makes it really difficult, because in our detective training, we're very based on paper, so we like physical crime scenes, we like talking to people, we like gathering the paper, we like taking away computers. The virtual world of the fraudster will require a virtual investigator. So whereas at the moment, you come to the operational teams, the vast majority will be operating like we've operated for many years. So we'll go out, take a statement, we'll go out and get the documentation, we'll go out and gather a computer. It's very tangible, very real. The reality is it's the virtual fraud where the big growth area is.
>
> **Q: Do you need a different skill set now as a fraud investigator?**
> **A:** I think you do, because I think the traditional skill sets of traditional investigators, it's about communication skills, it'll be about knowledge of law and procedure, it'll be about tenacity, it'll be about things that are fairly physical. I think for those going into the virtual world, you have to have a different skill set and a different mind. (EP11)

> Give us the tools, like with regard to the IT. Give us the knowledge, which is the biggest tool; we have a lot of self-teach packages, I think every force is similar. Because of the austerity measures, there isn't time for people to be away from the workplace to go and be trained in different issues. We need up-to-date training on IT, to understand the terminology, because victims are going to start coming to us and I'm going to be sat there with a blank face, which will be ineffective. I'm going to walk away thinking, 'I don't know what to do'. Give us the technology and cut the bureaucracy. (EP6)

Whilst technological advances left many police officers feeling that they were always one step behind organised criminals, others viewed cyber-enabled fraud as providing certain advantages to enforcement personnel.

> In some ways the internet has been a great help to us. Previously we'd know people were conspiring together but we wouldn't know what they'd said. Now you've got strings of emails and text messages on smart phones, what A has said to B, so that's been of benefit to us. But the best villains are more aware of that, there are things now where they can play an internet game like Call of Duty and have a conversation with another user, your opponent, but actually they're talking about their next job together, not the game. All kinds of social media, Skype too, where they can have offline conversations that we'll never get hold of. As a young detective I used to spend all day on the phone trying to get information. Now your phone never rings, everything's on email and where they use that, it helps us. Technology in terms of Bitcoins, the tools they have available, has changed everything … Malware for instance. We had a case recently involving the Bank of [name] where they managed to get a bit of Malware onto the computer and ended up getting someone's passwords so that they could get in and move money. (EP16)

For officers working in this area, the technological constraints they have to work with are an inevitable part of being a public sector body attempting to convict wealth-driven and asset-rich offenders.

Cultural Blindness: 'The Cinderella Crime'

A recurring view expressed by police interviewees was that police colleagues and the public view fraud as a low-priority offence when compared to other crimes such as drug trafficking and firearms, perhaps because many perceive it as a victimless crime. This criticism was levelled by officers—and by some offenders—at government officials, senior command teams, Police and Crime Commissioners, and the general public.

Officers consistently highlighted the need for fraud to be considered a serious crime due to the devastating impact it can have on victims. In a speech to the Financial Conduct Authority's (FCA) Financial Crime Conference in November 2016, the Conservative Home Secretary, Amber Rudd, stated that fraud is often referred to as 'the Cinderella crime'—in the shadows and overlooked. She highlighted that 'Fraud is the most prevalent crime in the country' and that 'serious and organised crime costs the UK at least £24 billion each year' (Rudd 2016). Regardless of the cost of fraud to individuals, institutions, and society, it is still viewed as a relatively minor, boring, and inconsequential crime, as highlighted below:

> We need to change the definition of fraud to incorporate money laundering because the minute you talk about fraud it's boring. When I was on the covert team we were doing the exciting stuff, surveillance of drug dealers, catching them with the gear, arresting them. In relation to fraud, they were in a different office and as an investigator you thought – boring. They took years to do anything, and we didn't, the two never met. Some of that still sticks – fraud is boring, it's slow, where's the real victim, who cares? (EP5)

All our police interviewees highlighted the need for fraud to be taken far more seriously by their colleagues, policy makers, and the public. Officer interviewees understood that fraud is rarely, if ever, a victimless crime and its impact seldom negligible but often considerable and life changing. All our offender interviewees had committed fraud over the value of £1 million. One interviewee believed his confiscation order would be between £100 and £300 million, illustrating the value and scale of the frauds he had committed; another interviewee described how within a week he had emptied a pensioner's bank account of her £70,000 savings; another was prosecuted for a £27m fraud that involved 4000 victims. All of our police interviewees described cases they or colleagues had worked on which involved vulnerable victims being defrauded of savings that were never seen again.

Whilst the cost of fraud to victims can be substantial, police interviewees believed that the perception of fraud as a 'victimless crime' predominates because the public believe that the banking and insurance industry *always* cover customers' losses and re-credit bank accounts of any monies fraudulently taken. Many of our police interviewees, however, described cases they had worked on where victims were duped by organised fraud groups into parting with considerable sums of money, with very little hope of recovering it. Particular types of fraud such as romance[3] and investment fraud are examples of frauds that rarely conclude with the victim being recompensed. Officers commented that when faced with a romance or investment fraud, the public's perception and in some cases the police perception turns from sympathy to one of contempt—often viewing the fraud victim as 'stupid', 'desperate', or 'greedy'. Such views were described by our police respondents as problematic and in many cases simply untrue. Nevertheless, the suggestion that a fraud victim is usually an unworthy victim predominates for many.

> It [investigating a case] means a lot to the victims, because they've lost large sums of money. And again, the perception of a lot of senior officers is that they were greedy to lose that amount of money. I would say, you know, and, and a lot of people looking in, would say, "How could they be so silly to lose all that money to a group of fraudsters?" But at the end of the day, they're just trying to make themselves that bit more money to have a more comfortable life, to look after their children and, and they've lost it all. (EP4)

> I think the main challenge is getting command teams interested in the work you're doing and appreciating the work you're doing. I think it is [acknowledged] in some respects but there's a middle level of management from detective inspector to superintendent who aren't involved in this crime support side. It frightens them to death, they're not interested and it seems like a waste of time; and, like I say, they think the victims are greedy or silly. (EP4)

In addition, victims of fraud can sometimes be unaware that they are the victim and/or reluctant to report a crime as fraud. In some cases, even when the crime is reported, officers fail to record the crime as fraud, preferring to re-define it as a regulatory matter or as something less serious (Button and Tunley 2015).

The fear of reputational damage for large financial and banking institutions was also highlighted as challenging for fraud investigators. Several interviewees highlighted the problematic situation which occurs when the fear of reputational damage leads to a lack of cooperation from the financial sector. For large financial institutions with international reputations to maintain being viewed as an 'easy hit' for organised fraudsters can be a devastating indictment of their security arrangements. Claude observed the positive impact a bank's denial can have on a sentence, and a financial investigator highlights the problems associated with working alongside the financial sector:

> The police said we had done at least £10 million, which we had; the banks denied it though. We were sentenced for £2.3million in the end. (Claude)

> Some financial institutions will not cooperate with regards to a criminal prosecution because once it goes to court it's in the public arena and their reputation can be damaged. They can lose customers or their share price falls. What's the answer to that? Perhaps government legislation to say, 'If you have been a victim of fraud you are compelled …' I mean they have to report suspicious activity to the bank, but it's up to them if they cooperate with an investigation'. (EP14)

Legislation to Tackle Organised Fraud: Asset Recovery, Money Laundering, and Post-conviction Court Orders

In an attempt to strengthen the response to organised criminality, the Labour government introduced the PoCA in 2002, which established the Asset Recovery Agency (ARA). The Act introduced new anti-money laundering and asset recovery powers[4] whilst strengthening the existing legislation relating to investigatory powers and restraint and confiscation procedures.[5] Part 7 of the Act also included a provision which requires businesses, within the regulated sectors (banks, solicitors, and accountancy firms), to report suspicious activity regarding money laundering by their customers and/or staff. The inclusion of this provision has, however, attracted criticism; opponents of the inclusion have highlighted that the Act has net widened the responsibility for the 'policing' of fraud and organised crime beyond the police; the new reality, in the eyes of the Act's critics, is that policing fraud is no longer the sole responsibility of the police.[6] Shortly after the introduction of PoCA (2002), the Serious Organised Crime and Policing Act 2005 (SOCPA) was passed. This particular Act aimed to complement the PoCA (2002) by strengthening the legislation post-conviction. In essence, its purpose was to enact arm's length financial surveillance once an offender has been released from prison or a community order is spent (Sproat 2009). To be able to do this the Act introduced two orders, the SCPO[7] and the FRO,[8] the aim of both being to curtail the criminal activities of offenders post-sentence.

Cram (2013) has argued that whilst 'PoCA legislation has provided frontline officers with an extended mandate to seize, detain and aggressively pursue forfeiture of any cash they come across in the line of duty' (2013:

128), there are evident gaps in the literature examining the impact of these increased police powers on frontline officers.

Sproat (2009) analysed four datasets:

(1) A Proceeds of Crime bulletin produced by the ARA
(2) Sentence lengths received by those convicted of money-laundering offences—data gathered by the Financial Action Task Force (FATF), the Home Office and Justice Office in Scotland
(3) Two tables about the value of cases dealt with by the ARA
(4) The number of FROs issued at the time of writing

Analysis of the results led Sproat to conclude that there was a degree of inaction by law enforcement agencies in their use of anti-money laundering and asset recovery powers. This view was supported by Edwards (2004: 30) who questioned 'whether the implementation gap reflects a gross overestimation of the proceeds of crime and/or poor performance on behalf of law enforcement agencies'.

Despite the Labour government's legislative focus on disrupting organised criminality, it would appear that the tools with which they equipped police professionals were and continue to be significantly underused. Research conducted by Sproat (2012) found that SCPOs were underused and that only a small numbers of offenders were convicted under SOCPA legislation. Sproat found that during the period 2006–2011, 1368 individuals were convicted under SOCPA legislation, which equates to around five percent of the estimated 25,000–30,000 individuals involved in organised crime in the UK.

During our interviews with offenders we asked whether an SCPO or an FRO had been imposed as part of their sentence. Consistent with Sproat's research, only two interviewees were subject to an SCPO, one of whom had appealed and had their order successfully quashed, and three offenders were subject to an FRO. Nearly all interviewees had, however, been served with a confiscation order; the amounts ranged from a car worth £60,000 to a house valued at £7 million (an alleged under-evaluation made by a professional enabler). One interviewee was waiting to hear about the amount to be confiscated but stated that it would be somewhere between £100 and £300 million, and a final interviewee had failed to pay his confiscation order and had 10 years added to his 17-year sentence. Most interviewees had also had numerous properties seized. Almost half (n = 13) of our interviewees had already had criminal property confiscated or a decision had been reached as to how much they owed as part of a confiscation order, and nine interviewees were either awaiting their confiscation hearing or for a decision to be made. Five interviewees said that as soon as the police started their investigation, their assets had been frozen. For example, Daley stated:

> I had a restraint order against my assets before they charged me, they froze my assets. Their argument was: 'now you're going to flog your assets'. (Daley)

Of the eight interviewees who had not had any criminal property confiscated, two explained that they had previously been pursued in civil cases against which assets were obtained, and as a result, there were no further assets to be recovered.

> Before the SFO trial I had already endured a civil case and had been stripped of all my assets and been declared bankrupt. There were no assets to confiscate. (Sven)

Three interviewees reported that they had been disqualified from holding a directorship for a specified period of time as part of their sentence. However, we learnt from our interview with Errol that he simply got round this element of his sentence by handing over his company to his business partner whilst he served his sentence and post-release working as a consultant.

Overall, our police interviewees were of the opinion that the PoCA (2002) was a welcome piece of legislation, assisting the police in their pursuit of criminal assets. However, several interviewees stated that whilst criminal property is pursued by the police as part of the investigation, in reality not much is recovered. One of the main challenges faced by asset recovery teams[9] is tracing money; money that can be dispersed across bank accounts and borders within a matter of minutes. Following the OCG, money trail was likened to 'chasing ghosts' by a number of our police interviewees.

> It's nice to get money back off criminals but does that stop them from committing more crime? Chances are they probably don't. Not if they're organised enough because you're never going to find the money in the first place. (EP31)

> We don't know where they [OCGs] are in the world … So, first of all, you've got to trace them. (EP6)

> Monies come in … I'll use a boiler room example, so the sale of unauthorised and worthless shares/assets, typically they would be laundered. They'd go through a central account and the monies would be dispersed to Hong Kong, British Virgin Islands and then perhaps come back into the UK under a different guise. But certainly, foreign jurisdictions in my experience, have been used to get the monies out. (EP14)

The difficulties associated with tracing the money were further compounded in cases where ill-gotten gains funded a 'champagne lifestyle'.

> It tends to be spent on living – you know, first class travel, top-end hotels, prestigious cars, the best of everything … If you've got high value vehicles that have been recovered, there's an opportunity [to seize assets] there. The same if it's gone into property. But, if it's just gone into living the lifestyle, then it's very difficult. That's always going to be part and parcel of the problem of asset recovery. (EP19)

Whilst a range of enforcement tools from confiscation orders to SCPOs are available, all of which are aimed at deterring involvement in organised crime, police interviewees highlighted a number of barriers to their use. Challenges included the difficulty of working on one case whilst monitoring offenders from previous cases post-release. Checking that offenders are complying with court orders was reported to be onerous, time consuming, and generally disruptive to an officer's day-to-day work. To avoid the burden of policing offenders post-release, officers tended to avoid applying to the courts for such orders. The high evidential standard required by judges when imposing orders was also seen as a barrier; in addition officers believed that there was a lack of awareness amongst officers compounded by a lack of available training on how the police and other legal practitioners could effectively use such orders.

> Attacking the assets is a brilliant tool which the Proceeds of Crime Act has brought in. It's one of the things the government has done well. If you're removing the benefits of committing crime, there's no point doing it in the first place. The problem is it's been a bit watered down and hence needs more resources putting into it. You get a confiscation order, there's no real way of enforcing it …. You need to be able to look again at his assets 10 years down the line when he's driving around in a flash car. Let's grab it then, but there's no real funding for it at the moment. (EP16)

> Administratively, it's quite a problem for us in the UK. It's not really sorted out and is reflected in the low numbers we have in place. (EP20)

> I don't know … whether there's enough resources put into looking at someone's bank statement for six months, which is an FRO. I think SCPOs are slightly better because they are specific and they are measurable in terms of you shouldn't do this or should do that. (EP15)

The Perceived Effectiveness of the Criminal Justice System: Views from the Other Side

We asked our offender interviewees about their views of the criminal justice system; as expected the answers were relatively varied. One interviewee claimed that being arrested had saved his life—'it literally saved my life', whilst others believed that the criminal justice system is inept at understanding the complexities of fraud cases 'enforcement officers don't know what they're enforcing, they don't know what they're looking for.' Others believed criminal justice employees, in particular lawyers, are uninterested in cases, preferring to assume that the defendant was guilty prior to a trial taking place: 'My lawyers were uninterested in my defence case … I was sweet-talked into pleading guilty.'

Despite their status as convicted offenders, none of our offender interviewees believed that enforcement agencies (including Police Forces, the National Crime Agency [NCA], Serious Fraud Office [SFO], and Her Majesty's Revenue and Customs [HMRC]) were effective at tackling OCGs involved in fraud. Few believed they had the resources, personnel, or 'know-how' to keep up with individuals intent on committing fraud. One interviewee, whilst scathing of the police, believed that enforcement activity will remain at a distinct disadvantage without the active cooperation of the financial/banking industry when preparing a case for court or investigating attacks on the banking and financial sector; this view was echoed by many of our police interviewees. Another interviewee believed that officers should be specially trained to investigate fraud, as illustrated below:

> They [the police] are fucking useless; they haven't got a fucking clue. I was running all over [city] out in the open. They didn't catch me I was grassed up. They haven't got a fucking chance, it's not their fault though, it's the banks, they keep everything from them; they are the real cunts in all of this. (Claude)

Enforcement officers don't know what they're enforcing, they don't know what they're looking for. The people setting the laws and enforcing them don't understand the business. Rules and regulations need to be in place and complied with. Enforcement officers should be made to a) pass their own exams and b) be experienced [in investigating fraud]. (Cyril)

Interviewer: Do you think enforcement activity is effective at detecting OC fraudulent activity?
Interviewee: No, They've still got no clue what they're doing. I could wipe out that industry in six months. They are doing it all the wrong way, wrong mentality. Capture a few to scare off the majority. Put it to bed, but it drives it underground. What they need to be doing is stopping it, so that the investor doesn't lose the money in the first place. (Max)

Views of the CPS and Trial by Jury

Given the seriousness of the cases against all our interviewees, none were eligible to be dealt with by a Magistrates' Court. All but one interviewee pleaded not guilty, resulting in 30 of our 31 interviewees being tried by a jury; all 31 were subsequently sentenced by a Crown Court judge. All of those that were tried by a jury expressed dissatisfaction with the process and held the view that their juries were unable to understand the complexities involved in their fraud case, were bored by the evidence, and 'switched off' due to the length of the trial, as illustrated below:

No one [on the jury] understood accounting practices or could even come close to identifying with the pressures of being [in the financial industry]. We were left [on the jury] with a few housewives, a few unemployed people and a student. They saw a kid who's 32, earns £350,000 a year, who was just as corrupt as the others ... They would never have understood. (Dexter)

You need specialist lawyers to understand the complexity and specialist juries and judges. It is a battle of hearts and minds. What is dishonesty in an environment where everyone is dishonest? (Dexter)

Interviewer: Did the jury understand the complexity of what was being put to them?
Interviewee: Absolutely not. They didn't know what a treasury bond was. It [the trial] was 18 weeks. They were falling asleep. I had to bang on the glass to wake them up. There were days and days of barristers on their feet

talking paperwork. They bored everyone. They [the jury] would have missed evidence. There were eight barristers; they [the jury] had to hear that evidence eight times. (Reggie)

Being part of an OCG is considered an aggravating factor at court and if proven is taken into consideration by a judge when sentencing. Twenty-one interviewees stated that the CPS had put to the judge (and where relevant a jury) that the defendant was part of an OCG, nine stated that it had not been mentioned, and one stated that the CPS prosecutor intimated that he was part of an OCG but did not unequivocally state it; the final interviewee failed to answer the question. Of those interviewees who disputed being part of an OCG, many were particularly disgruntled by the description assigned to them by the CPS; others saw the description as a badge of honour, and the remainder were slightly bewildered by the label, as illustrated below:

The prosecution said I was highly organised, audacious and totally professional. (Terry)

They basically said it was organised crime dressed up as a genuine business. Boiler room has become a catchphrase. (Max)

That's what they put it down to yeah [being part of an OCG]. There were three victims who were old, about 70 plus, the rest were under 60. They [CPS] said we were targeting the old and vulnerable. They read out my [incriminating] text messages to my co-defendants in court. (George)

I'm not sure how they convinced the jury that I was part of an organised crime group. (Sandra)

Yes, that's exactly what they said [that interviewee was part of an OCG], because the police officers decided to make it so. (Reggie)

Whilst one interviewee stated that the CPS had not described him at court as part of an OCG, he went on to state that 'a criminal lifestyle was intimated and that I was head of a team of three'.

Prison Associations and Networks

As part of the interview, we asked interviewees whether they had maintained any contact with their co-defendants/networks post-trial. Whilst none of our interviewees disclosed any criminal activity whilst in prison and some interviewees stated that they had only met their co-defendant at the trial, a surprising number were either sharing a cell with one of their co-defendants or were in the same prison establishment. This would seem to suggest that prisons—possibly due to capacity issues—are unable to disrupt networks that are keen to keep operating post-sentence. Other interviewees, however, had not been in contact with their co-defendants since their trial, as illustrated below:

I've got my networks in place, if I wanted to I suppose it's all still there, but I'm not going back to it. (Claude)

> **Interviewer:** What impact do you think a prison sentence has on pre-existing networks/associations?
> **Interviewee:** Nothing. I've spent my entire sentence with my co-defendants. I've been approached on numerous occasions to 'collaborate' with others once I'm out; they're not in my league though. (Terry)

> I spend more time with one of them [co-defendant] than any other human being, he's my cell mate. (Carter)

> I still have contact with three of my co-defendants. They're now at a Cat D,[10] I'm a year behind them. (Max)

> All my previous relationship have been negated, I have a few close friends left. People like me don't have friends. (Cyril)

In Conclusion

This chapter has examined the policing and sentencing of organised fraud, mainly from the perspective of policing professionals. We found that fraud investigations involving OCGs tended to be relatively complex and were reported to take many months/years to reach a conclusion. At a local level, setting priorities appeared to be relatively fluid; regional and local teams tended to examine the merits of each case to then decide whether or not to investigate. One recurring commonality on whether to investigate/prioritise or not was vulnerability of the victim. The importance of containing and focusing investigations was viewed as significant. Deciding on an investigation's parameters as soon as practicable often created the best possible chance of achieving a successful result on behalf of the victim(s). The complexity of investigations, in particular cross-border/jurisdiction cases, the threat posed by new technologies, resource issues, and the problems associated with the low priority fraud is often afforded were issues highlighted by our enforcement interviewees as everyday difficulties. The speed with which organised criminals adapt their business practices leaves the police with very little choice but to react to criminal activity rather than proactively try to prevent it.

Only two interviewees were subject to an SCPO as part of their sentence. FROs were attached to the sentences of three interviewees. Interviewees reported confiscation figures which ranged from a token £1 payment to estimates between £100 and £300 million in assets. Five interviewees said that as soon as the police started their investigation, their assets had been frozen. No interviewee believed that enforcement agencies (including Police Forces, NCA, SFO, HMRC) were effective at tackling OCGs involved in fraud and nearly expressed dissatisfaction with the trial by jury process and held the view that juries were singly unable to understand the complexities involved in fraud cases, were bored by the evidence, and often 'switched off' due to the length of the trial. Whilst none of our interviewees disclosed any criminal activity whilst in prison, a surprising number were either sharing a cell with one of their co-defendants or were in the same prison establishment.

Notes

1. Action Fraud is the reporting function of the National Fraud Intelligence Bureau (NFIB), which holds national responsibility for taking fraud reports.
2. At the time of research, FROs were an order in their own right; however, following the Serious Crime Act 2015, the FRO was subsumed into the SCPO and now forms part of this order.
3. 'A romance fraud occurs when you think you've met the perfect partner through an online dating website or app, but the other person is using a fake profile to form a relationship with you. They're using the site to gain your trust and ask you for money or enough personal information to steal your identity'. (Action Fraud) http://www.actionfraud.police.uk/fraud_protection/dating_fraud.
4. The College of Policing Authorise Professional Practice states that: 'Asset recovery makes sure that crime does not pay by seizing and confiscating assets acquired by individuals as a result of crime, such as cash, property, vehicles and high-value goods. A large proportion of the money received by the government as a result of asset recovery is then given back to the law enforcement agencies as an incentive towards recovering assets and to help reduce crime further.' https://www.app.college.police.uk/app-content/

investigations/investigative-strategies/financial-investigation-2/asset-recovery/.

5. Confiscation is defined thus: 'Confiscation is where an individual convicted of committing a crime is also suspected to have benefited financially from that crime and legal action is taken to confiscate the assets acquired from criminal activity. The role of the confiscation process is to recover the value of the assets that have benefited that individual, such as cash, properties or vehicles. This value can be recovered following a successful conviction by applying to the court for a confiscation order. If the order is granted the court will assess which assets can be confiscated, and the value of those assets.' (College of Policing APP, https://www.app.college.police.uk/app-content/investigations/investigative-strategies/financial-investigation-2/asset-recovery/).
6. Unfortunately, the Agency failed to meet its targets so was merged with the Serious Organised Crime Agency in 2008 (which later became the National Crime Agency).
7. The SCPO was introduced by the SOCPA 2005. An individual must have been convicted of a serious offence (including fraud, money laundering, and organised crime) by the Crown Court for an order to be attached post-conviction. Requirements of an SCPO include restrictions on financial, property, or business dealings; communication with certain individuals; travel both within UK and abroad; and the use of certain items. An order can also require a person to answer questions or provide information or documents specified in the order.
8. Prior to 2015, when convicted of a serious offence (including fraud, theft, money laundering, and funding terrorism), a court was able to impose an FRO on an offender post-conviction. The order required an individual to report to the police on his or her financial circumstances. Information requested could include details of income, assets, credit card accounts, financial transactions, and tax returns. FROs now form part of an SCPO, having been incorporated into the Serious Crime Act 2015.
9. 'An Asset Recovery Team primarily seeks to dismantle and disrupt serious and organised crime through the confiscations of financial proceeds obtained from criminal conduct. The nature of investigations undertaken often involves serious and complex fraud cases.' (City of London Police) https://www.cityoflondon.police.uk/advice-and-support/fraud-and-economic-crime/fraudsquads/Pages/Asset-recovery-team.aspx.
10. A Cat D refers to a Category D prison, which is an open prison. If approved, prisoners in a Cat D are given a 'Release On Temporary Licence' to work in the community or to go on home leave once they have passed their Full Licence Eligibility Dates, which tends to be a quarter of the way through the sentence.

References

Button, M. (2011). Fraud Investigation and the 'Flawed Architecture' of Counter Fraud Entities in the United Kingdom. *International Journal of Law, Crime and Justice, 39*, 249–265.

Button, M., & Tunley, M. (2015). Explaining Fraud Deviancy Attenuation in the United Kingdom. *Crime, Law and Social Change, 63*(1–2), 49–64.

Button, M., Johnston, L., Frimpong, K., & Smith, G. (2007). New Directions in Policing Fraud: The Emergence of the Counter Fraud Specialist in the United Kingdom. *International Journal of the Sociology of Law, 35*, 192–208.

Cram, F. (2013). Understanding the Proceeds of Crime Act 2002: Cash Seizure and Frontline Policing. *The Howard Journal of Criminal Justice, 52*(2), 121–131.

Doig, A., & Levi, M. (2013). A Case of Arrested Development? Delivering the UK National Fraud Strategy Within Competing Policing Policy Priorities. *Public Money & Management, 33*(2), 145–152.

Doig, A., Johnson, S., & Levi, M. (2001). New Public Management, Old Populism and the Policing of Fraud. *Public Policy and Administration, 16*, 9.

Edwards, A. (2004). Understanding Organised Crime. *Criminal Justice Matters, 55*(1), 30–31.

Finckenauer, J. O. (2005). Problems of Definition: What Is Organized Crime? *Trends in Organized Crime, 8*, 63–83.

Fraud Advisory Panel. (2016). *The Fraud Review—Ten Years On* [Online]. Available at: https://www.fraudadvisorypanel.org/wp-content/uploads/2016/06/The-Fraud-Review-Ten-Years-On-WEB.pdf. Accessed 5 Apr 2017.

Harfield, C. (2008). The Organization of 'Organized Crime Policing' and Its International Context. *Criminology & Criminal Justice, 8*(4), 483–507.

HM Government. (2006). *Fraud Review: Final Report.* London: Home Office.

Home Office. (2012). *The Strategic Policing Requirement.* London: Home Office.

Levi, M., & Burrows, J. (2008). Measuring the Impact of Fraud in the UK: A Conceptual and Empirical Journey. *British Journal of Criminology, 48*(3), 293–318.

ONS. (2016). Crime in England and Wales: Year Ending Sept 2016 [Online]. Available at: https://www.ons.gov.uk/peoplepopulationandcommunity/crimeandjustice. Accessed 26 Apr 2017.

Penna, S., & Kirby, S. (2013). Bridge Over the River Crime: Mobility and the Policing of Organised Crime. *Mobilities*, 8(4), 487–505.

Rudd, A. (2016). *Home Secretary's Speech to the FCA's Financial Crime Conference* [Online]. Available at: https://www.gov.uk/government/speeches/home-secretarys-speech-to-the-fcas-financial-crime-conference. Accessed 12 May 2017.

Sproat, P. (2009). To What Extent Is the UK's Anti-Money Laundering and Asset Recovery Regime Used Against Organised Crime? *Journal of Money Laundering Control, 12*(2), 134–150.

Sproat, P. (2012). Phoney War or Appeasement? The Policing of Organised Crime in the UK. *Trends in Organized Crime, 15*, 313–330. https://doi.org/10.1007/s12117-012-9154-4.

CHAPTER 6

Concluding Thoughts

Abstract This chapter provides a summary of the main findings of the report, highlighting the many routes into fraud, the diversity of the individuals involved in this type of criminality, the differing structures supporting the numerous organised crime groups (OCGs), and a comprehensive examination of the policing of organised criminals. The chapter emphasises that whilst rapid solutions are not on the horizon, it is important that the many agencies involved continue to tackle OCGs energetically and on several fronts. Recommendations put forward include tackling misperceptions that fraud by OCGs is victimless; improving awareness regarding the role of professional enablers and the risk factors that predict their recruitment to OCGs; encouraging enforcement professionals to apply for and enforce the full range of Policing and Organised Crime Act (POCA) Orders; assembling a more nuanced understanding of professional enablers, money launderers, and identity criminals; and finally highlighting the importance of horizon scanning.

Keywords Capable guardianship • Professional enablers • Criminal sanctions • Information sharing • Partnership work • Victimless crime

This book has aimed to characterise organised criminals involved in fraud and outline the complexities of tackling these groups. We have shown that

T. May, B. Bhardwa, *Organised Crime Groups involved in Fraud*,
Crime Prevention and Security Management,
https://doi.org/10.1007/978-3-319-69401-6_6

there are many routes into organised fraud, many different individuals involved in this type of criminality, and numerous structures supporting these groups. Different sorts of organised crime group (OCG) and forms of offending will demand different sorts of response. Traditionally, tackling OCGs has been the exclusive responsibility of specialist officers and, to a degree, specialist agencies within the criminal justice system. Other agencies have not been expected or required to respond to organised criminality and until recently have not been part of the broader enforcement and prevention landscape. As we shall argue, some OCGs will be tackled effectively only if responsibility for doing so is spread broadly across a number of agencies. Whilst *rapid* solutions are not on the horizon, in this chapter we argue that it is still important to tackle OCGs energetically and on several fronts.

We shall examine options for tackling OCGs involved in fraud, looking specifically at:

- Capable guardianship and the role of professional enablers
- Encouraging the greater use of criminal sanctions
- Consolidating, sharing, and acting upon information and data
- Tackling the misperception that organised fraud is a victimless crime

First, however, we shall summarise the key findings to have emerged from our study.

Routes into Organised Fraud

The routes into fraud and organised crime followed by our respondents were diverse and complex. At one end of the spectrum were those who were recruited and unintentionally drawn in by OCGs and at the other end were those who made an intentional and conscious choice to become involved in organised crime and fraud. The majority of interviewees, however, made a conscious decision to engage in organised fraud and were driven by financial gain. Some committed fraud by exploiting loopholes within legitimate occupations; others did it by building it into business plans and actively seeking fraud out as a way of making money; others were either involved politically or had political connections and used these positions and networks to facilitate their route into organised economic crime. The remainder's route into organised fraud was through either 'targeted' or 'serendipitous' recruitment by existing OCGs.

Professional enablers were invaluable to OCGs; they opened doors that would otherwise be closed to such groups to facilitate criminal activity. Solicitors, accountants, financial advisers, bank managers, and mortgage brokers all assisted the criminal activity of our interviewees, in addition to bank clerks, staff at retail outlets, postal workers, firemen, doormen, and casino staff.

The Nature and Structure of OCGs Involved in Fraud

The police officers we interviewed suggested that OCGs involved in fraud take on a variety of organisational structures. Organised fraudsters were described by some police officers as often older, from an educated or professional background, and with little or no prior criminal involvement. This profile was associated with what they viewed as the classic OCG structure: hierarchical and pyramidical in form. Other police officers argued that a slightly different structure had emerged, one which was characterised by loose, slightly more dynamic networks of offenders who work together in a synchronised and complementary way to commit fraud. These police officers argued that the perception of the classic fraudster is eroding and becoming somewhat outdated. Another OCG structure was the global network structure; this followed a similar business model to the classic structure but operated at a European and an international level. Another derivative of the classic OCG structure was characterised by a hierarchical top tier and fluid or chaotic lower tiers. There were also those who committed fraud as part of smaller OCGs in which power was almost evenly distributed amongst co-conspirators. In many respects the classic, hierarchical structure was the most dominant, but it had adapted to account for the geographical spread of OCG operations across borders and for different types of organised fraud.

Policing Organised Fraudsters

A recurring theme to emerge from the offender interviews was the ease with which organised fraudsters were able to commit fraud. For many, manipulating loopholes and understanding the system they defrauded, in conjunction with the assistance provided by professional enablers, allowed them to commit fraud for a number of years before any wrong-doing was detected. From the enforcement perspective, police interviewees noted that fraud investigations involving OCGs tended to be relatively complex and could take many months or years to reach a conclusion. The complexity of investigations, in particular cross-border/jurisdiction cases, the threat posed by new technologies, resource issues, and the problems associated with the low priority fraud is often afforded were highlighted by our enforcement interviewees as everyday difficulties. The vulnerability of the victim was frequently a consideration in decisions on whether to investigate. The speed with which organised criminals were able to adapt their business practices often left the police with very little choice but to react to criminal activity rather than to try to prevent it proactively.

One of the main challenges faced by asset recovery teams was the difficulty of tracing money that had been dispersed across bank accounts and borders within a matter of minutes. Only two of the offender interviewees were subject to a Serious Crime Prevention Order (SCPO) as part of their sentence and three had been issued with a Financial Reporting Order (FRO). Interviewees reported confiscation figures which ranged from a token £1 payment to estimates ranging from £100 to £300 million in assets. Whilst none of our interviewees disclosed any criminal activity whilst in prison, a surprising number were either sharing a cell with one of their co-defendants or were in the same prison establishment.

Capable Guardianship and the Role of Professional Enablers

The role of professional enablers in OCGs is beginning to receive recognition, as is the importance of targeting preventive efforts on them. Growing interest in the role played by professionals as 'gatekeepers' (World Economic Forum 2012) in enabling organised crime has been reflected in the UK government's organised crime strategies. The Serious and Organised Crime Strategy (2013) highlighted the potential impact of professionals (e.g. lawyers, accountants, and bankers) in facilitating organised criminality:

> *Organised criminals very often depend on the assistance of corrupt, complicit or negligent professionals, notably lawyers, accountants and bankers.* (Home Office 2013: 14)

The importance of professional enablers to OCGs was highlighted again in the later National Strategic Assessment of Serious and Organised Crime 2015:

> *Those involved in serious and organised crime work in groups or as individuals and seek to exploit vulnerabilities through a range of activities including, for example, taking advantage of legislative loopholes, bribery and corruption and employment of professional enablers such as criminally complicit solicitors or letting agents.* (NCA 2015: 8)

However, recognition of the importance of enablers' roles is likely to remain at an abstract level, without any serious commitment to take preventative action, so long as information about enablers remains so thin. This book has restricted its area of study to OCGs involved in fraud; our findings need testing and extending to other forms of organised criminality. We believe, however, that an important step in mobilising resources against enablers is to ensure that politicians, senior enforcement professionals, and those in the regulatory bodies that oversee professionals have a much more concrete and textured understanding of enablers and the role they play within OCGs. If information of this sort helps to generate energy for change and promote capable guardianship, we believe it is also important to review the range of preventative approaches that can be deployed, such as:

- Early identification of people at risk of involvement in organised crime
- Better targeting of resources to charge and prosecute enablers

Early Identification of People at Risk of Involvement in Organised Crime

Early identification of those at risk of recruitment to OCGs is an essential element of the Government's 'Prevent' strand of the Serious and Organised Crime Strategy (2013). The objectives are to:

- Deter people from becoming involved in serious and organised crime by raising awareness of the reality and consequences
- Use interventions to stop people being drawn into different types of serious and organised crime
- Develop techniques to deter people from continuing in serious and organised criminality
- Establish an effective offender management framework to support work on Pursue and Prevent (Home Office 2013: 45)

Understanding how and in what way organised criminals infiltrate the legal and financial professions is essential if successful protective and regulatory measures are to be implemented. Identifying where the weaknesses are in the system cannot be achieved simply by reviewing the prosecution figures. At present we still have only rudimentary knowledge about the recruitment of professionals to OCGs, their knowledge of the organised criminality they are part of, if and how they may facilitate or cover up identity theft, and the tactics taken thereafter by professionals to avoid detection. Information of this sort is needed to raise professional awareness of the risks posed by organised criminals and to deter those who are most likely to be drawn in. Both regulators and enforcement professionals need to narrow the opportunities open to organised criminals to co-opt professionals.

Better Targeting of Resources to Charge and Prosecute Enablers

We have shown that professional enablers are rarely the focus of organised crime investigations as limited enforcement resources tend to be targeted on those offenders who appear to cause the most harm, and on seizing their assets. The enforcement philosophy, understandably, is to target those who are the prime movers of OCGs. However, disrupting the activities of professional enablers may be equally effective. The case for doing so is strengthened by research from the Solicitors Regulatory Authority (SRA) and the National Crime Agency showing that enablers sometimes play a central role in organised crime and do not simply have walk-on parts into which they have been duped or coerced (SRA 2014: 6). In tackling those professionals at the more serious end of criminality, the new powers of prohibiting involvement in activities that support OCGs, introduced by the 2015 Serious Crime Act, may facilitate effective use of scarce resources. As yet, no published research exists which has assessed whether realigning resources to target professionals is a workable proposition and whether it will yield the desired result of disrupting the activities of organised criminals. We therefore need a better understanding of the relationships between the regulatory bodies and enforcement professionals, their preparedness to cooperate, and the challenges that such cooperation may present. The views of both groups need to be sought about the feasibility and desirability of a refocusing of effort and funding on enablers within OCGs.

Encouraging the Greater Use of Criminal Sanctions

The Proceeds of Crime Act 2002 (PoCA) saw the 'mainstreaming' of police cash seizure powers aimed at disrupting serious, organised crime (Cram 2013: 121). The Act contained new anti-money laundering and asset recovery powers. Additional provisions were included in the Serious and Organised Crime and Policing Act 2005 (SOCPA) which provided for the financial scrutiny of serious organised criminals post-conviction (Sproat 2009: 135). Research conducted by Sproat (2009) highlighted the 'inaction' of law enforcement agencies in their use of anti-money laundering and asset recovery powers. Following Sproat's research, our findings also suggest that there is a distinct underuse of the SCPO, which has now subsumed the FRO. Despite an absence of research examining the use and effectiveness of the existing orders, new provisions have been introduced under the Serious Crime Act 2015. In our view it is important to identify the reasons for the underuse of the earlier post-conviction orders and to establish early sight-lines on the operation of the new 2015 provisions. For post-conviction orders to be successful there must be adequate systems in place to evaluate the appropriateness of their application and the impact on the behaviour of offenders. Understanding the reluctance of enforcement professionals to apply for such orders is also an essential component of improving their use.

Consolidating, Sharing, and Acting upon Information and Data

As mentioned in Chap. 1, traditional perceptions of organised crime and the types of criminality associated with it have evolved. The Internet and advances in technology have created new, innovative, and easier ways to commit fraud and for offenders to dupe and defraud individual victims, public sector services, and large corporations. Our findings have highlighted that fraud is easy to commit, lucrative, and almost risk free. Put simply, it is likely to become a crime of choice for both lone offenders and OCGs, in particular because the likelihood of actually getting caught is relatively slim.

Partnerships between the police, corporate, commercial, and public bodies exist. The joint work currently being undertaken is welcomed by all of the agencies involved; indeed, many of our police interviewees discussed the partnerships as positive, effective, and beneficial. However, given the fast-paced nature of economic crime, future partnership work might benefit from a more systematic and transparent approach and a greater scrutiny of the effectiveness of the range of approaches taken, which may require additional legislation.

To be able to map trends, horizon scan, and measure effectiveness in a timely and effectual manner, there is a growing argument that mandatory reporting by the banks to Action Fraud needs to be introduced. Reporting should be for all cases of theft and fraud over a particular threshold, and reports should include details of the amount, modus operandi, and details of the receiving bank. Mapping in this way would allow the police and banking industry to scan for new threats and get a clearer sense of the current problems. Effective deterrents and solutions will be achievable only when both the banking industry and enforcement professionals are much better sighted on vulnerabilities and weaknesses. Such a database will inevitably allow enforcement professionals to mount proactive as well as reactive investigations and will also provide the banking industry with a clearer picture of how and where their weaknesses are being exploited.

Following on from mapping trends, the banking industry should perhaps seek to evaluate their current arrangements for alerting customers to atypical transactions. Presently, the system identifies some, but by no means all, unusual transactions; it would appear that there needs to be a consistent and more rigorous process of querying large and unusual transaction if banks are to avoid organised fraudsters stealing vast sums of money which leave the county within a matter of minutes. Attempting to trace such money was referred to, by our enforcement professionals, as 'chasing ghosts'.

Less Can Sometimes Be More

Whilst much is made of the banks protecting their customers, customers also need to take responsibility for their accounts. To help customers achieve this, the banking industry needs to look for ways to improve how best they warn people of the real risks they face. The general public receive numerous flyers, emails, free offers, and catalogues from a range of companies, and many people feel as if they are the victims of information overload, drowning in irrelevant, extraneous, and unimportant material. The banking industry may benefit from carefully selecting what marketing material is emailed and posted to customers and research whether customers would benefit from a pithy, jargon-free 'risks and warnings' leaflet/

email or text. For information to have currency, it needs to stand out from the crowd and not be just another leaflet to recycle or unopened email to delete.

Tackling the Misperception That Organised Fraud Is a Victimless Crime

The impact of organised fraud is widespread; fraudsters create victims of individuals, businesses, public sector services, and private industry. Despite the scale of fraud, it is still perceived by many—including the public, police service, and fraudsters themselves—as a victimless crime. There are a number of reasons why this is the case, many of which we have highlighted in this book. The two most damaging falsehoods are:

- Victims are recompensed so there is no 'real' victim.
- Fraud victims are not real victims; they are simply victims of their own 'stupidity' and 'greed'.

'The Victim Is Recompensed'

Both our offender and police interviewees suggested that fraud is often viewed as a victimless crime because in many cases, fearful of reputational damage, the banks and insurance industry simply recompense fraud victims, writing off their losses and essentially, in doing so, eliminating 'the victim'.

ATM fraudster Simon provided his rationale for committing this particular type of crime:

> There are other easier frauds but I don't want to get involved because there are bigger sentences. Also, the money we steal, everyone gets it back. The banks are happy to be defrauded because they can claim their losses back from insurance. (Simon)

In contrast to this view, police interviewees described cases in which fraud victims were unable to recover any of their losses and some only a fraction. Encouraging police professionals to seize and freeze assets at the earliest opportunity and apply for SCPOs to disable future fraud plans is one way to tackle the issue of victims who fail to be recompensed. For those that are, the onus to report the fraud falls to individual banks (or affected industry). Mandatory reporting—as suggested above—would avoid losses being glossed over and assist in eradicating the view that fraud is a victimless crime.

'Fraud Victims Are Not Real Victims; They Are Victims of Their Own Stupidity and Greed'

Fraud is an underreported crime; sometimes this is the result of the banking and financial industry recompensing victims and then failing to report the fraud and subsequent loss to the police. At other times it can be the result of victims feeling and being perceived as unworthy, stupid, or greedy, all of which can be powerful motivators to remain silent. Changing ingrained perceptions is a complex and difficult task; however, fraud is a growth industry, and misperceptions and misinformation need to be challenged.

With the recent inclusion of fraud in the Crime Survey for England and Wales, now more than ever before, the capacity exists to develop a much better insight into fraud and its victims and to pass this information to those implementing the ongoing programme of work with the public. Raising 'awareness of the reality and consequences' (Home Office 2013) forms a key component of the 'Prevent' strand of the Serious and Organised Crime Strategy. Whilst this work is ongoing, an evaluation might be timely. An evaluation of the impact this work is having and the usefulness and appropriateness of the approach across sectors and across online and offline platforms needs to be examined if the status and view of victims is to change.

And Finally

Fraud, along with many other crimes, has, over the last 20 years, adapted to the increasingly online world that most of us now inhabit. With more of our lives being conducted online (e.g. shopping, dating, social interactions, reading, and playing games), the greater the distance between offender and victim can be (e.g. cyber bullying, sexual exploitation, fraud, theft, stalking, and harassment). In short, offenders have the ability to commit their crime of choice without being seen or heard. Nearly all of the frauds discussed in this book were able to be committed without the offender coming into contact with the victim. This lack of contact inadvertently promotes the idea that fraud is not only a lesser crime compared to other crimes such as robbery, but also a faceless crime. However, fraud can and often does have a life-changing impact on victims and needs to be tackled energetically on a number of fronts by both the police and their partner agencies.

References

Cram, F. (2013). Understanding the Proceeds of Crime Act 2002: Cash Seizure and Frontline Policing. *The Howard Journal of Criminal Justice, 52*(2), 121–131.

Home Office. (2013). *Serious and Organised Crime Strategy*. London: Home Office.

NCA. (2015). *National Strategic Assessment of Serious and Organised Crime 2015*. National Crime Agency.

Sproat, P. (2009). To What Extent Is the UK's Anti-Money Laundering and Asset Recovery Regime Used Against Organised Crime? *Journal of Money Laundering Control, 12*(2), 134–150.

SRA. (2014). *Cleaning Up: Law Firms and the Risk of Money Laundering*. Solicitor's Regulation Authority. Available at: http://www.sra.org.uk/risk/resources/risk-money-laundering.page

World Economic Forum. (2012). *Organised Crime Enablers: Global Agenda Council on Organized Crime*. World Economic Forum. Available at: http://reports.weforum.org/organized-crime-enablers-2012/

Appendix A: Taking Stock of Organised Crime: Analysis of National Organised Crime Group Mapping Data

The main questions that the research sought to answer were:

- How do the characteristics of known organised crime groups (OCGs) involved in fraud-related offences differ from others?
- Among known OCGs, what factors best predict involvement in organised forms of fraud?

Key Findings

- Analysis of anonymised organised crime group mapping (OCGM) data identified over 4800 OCGs (who could be linked to at least one crime type and whose details could be disseminated) and more than 33,000 individuals (or nominals) mapped by agencies in England, Wales, and Northern Ireland; 34% of these criminal enterprises were involved in fraud-related activities. Our analysis examined the characteristics of those groups considered to be engaged in high levels of fraud-related criminality (7%), relative to other (low or medium criminality) fraud groups (27%) and all other (non-fraud) OCGs (66%).
- Fraud-related OCGs were considered to have intent and capability across a wider range of areas, including in relation to expertise, infiltration, corruption, and subversion, involvement in multiple enterprises, resistance and/or resilience, and cash flow. By contrast, they

T. May, B. Bhardwa, *Organised Crime Groups involved in Fraud*,
Crime Prevention and Security Management,
https://doi.org/10.1007/978-3-319-69401-6

were less likely to display violent capability, have links with other OCGs, or be considered tactically aware. Similarly, those engaged in high levels of fraud-related criminality—in contrast to those mapped with low/medium levels of criminality in this area—were considered to have intent and capability across a larger number of areas. This was true with regard to infiltration, corruption, and subversion, growth potential, expertise, resistance/resilience, involvement in multiple enterprises, and cash flow. They were, however, significantly less likely to display violent capability relative to other (low/medium criminality) fraud groups.

- Intent and capability scores derived from OCGM were significantly higher for those groups engaged in high and low/medium levels of fraud-related criminality, when compared to non-fraud OCGs.
- While there was no difference between fraud-related OCGs and others in terms of the average number of known members operating within these groups, they tended to have proportionally fewer male nominals, be of an older average age, and were less likely to be British nationals. Compared to other fraud-related criminal enterprises and non-fraud OCGs, those groups engaged in high levels of fraud-related criminality were significantly less likely to comprise male offenders, they were older in age, and they were more likely to be non-British nationals.
- Relative to those engaged in low/medium levels of fraud-related criminality and non-fraud OCGs, those criminal enterprises mapped as having high levels of fraud-related criminality were significantly more likely to have an international dimension and be expanding their enterprises through UK borders, be considered to have a recognised structure, and have estimated assets in excess of £1 million.
- Fraud-related OCGs were less likely to have links with other criminal enterprises, but were involved in more areas of criminality (particularly those groups with a high level of fraud-related criminality). There were strong correlations observed between involvement in economic crime and specialist money laundering, commodity importation, counterfeiting or illegal supply, cyber and environmental crime. By contrast, those OCGs engaged in economic crime were significantly less likely to also be involved in drugs activity, violent crime, and organised theft.
- When compared to other criminal enterprises, fraud-related OCGs were significantly more likely to be reported via the mapping process as having an exceptional level of criminality, a pivotal role in enabling

substantial criminality among other OCGs, some criminal activities not being assessed, political/reputational damage arising from their activities, and an impact upon a community to an exceptional level. These differences were largely driven by those engaged in high levels of fraud-related criminality. In contrast to other fraud-related groups, these particular criminal enterprises were considered to be engaged in an exceptional level of criminality, play a pivotal role in enabling substantial criminality among other groups, have potential for considerable political/reputational damage arising from their offending; and have key elements of their offending unassessed using the current mapping framework.

- Fraud-related OCGs were more likely to incorporate a regulated occupation or specialist role, and have more of these specialist roles present within their groups. Regulated occupations were also more likely to be reported within those groups engaged in high levels of fraud-related criminality, in contrast to other fraud groups, and they had more specialist roles present within them.
- Mapped OCGs engaged in fraud had links with more companies and were more likely to be linked to them in the capacity of an owner, manager, or operative. Compared to other OCGs, the legitimate companies to which fraud-related criminal enterprises were linked were also significantly more likely to be complicit in facilitating serious crime, laundering, and acting as a front to import/export goods. Those engaged in high levels of fraud-related criminality had links with more companies than other (low/medium criminality) fraud OCGs, but with no significant differences between them in the way in which they were linked to these companies. Compared to other fraud OCGs, the legitimate companies to which these high criminality fraud groups had links were significantly more likely to be acting as a front to import/export goods, be complicit in laundering, and facilitating serious crime.
- OCGs engaged in fraud-related activities were more likely to have an identifiable link with business, in particular professional services and other (unspecified) sectors. Conversely, they were less likely to have links with the catering and health/beauty sectors. Those engaged in high levels of fraud-related criminality were significantly more likely to be linked with other (unspecified) business sectors than other fraud-related OCGs, but less likely to have links with the environmental sector.

- Fraud-related OCGs were significantly more likely to use technological services for criminal purposes or to enable involvement in crime, to use the Internet as an enabler, and to be engaged in a specific Internet- or technology-enabled crime type. In contrast to other fraud OCGs, those involved in a high level of fraud-related criminality were more likely to exploit technological services for criminal purposes or to facilitate involvement in crime, and use the Internet as an enabler.
- The results of multivariate analysis of OCGM data indicate that the key features which distinguished OCGs engaged in a high level of fraud-related criminality from others were having estimated assets in excess of £1 million, generating significant political/reputational damage arising from their activities, having an international dimension, using technological services for criminal purposes, having a regulated occupation within their ranks, an identifiable link with the business sector, playing a pivotal role in enabling substantial criminality among other OCGs, and involvement in other areas of criminality. By contrast, they were significantly less likely to be British or involved in multiple enterprises.

Data Source

The analysis drew upon an anonymised extract of data derived from the OCGM process. The data were extracted from returns made by forces and organisations across England, Wales, and Northern Ireland, relating to 7448 OCGs.[1] The analysis was restricted to data relating to 4824 OCGs for whom details on criminality type were reported to the OCGM. This included both active (82.9%) and archived (17.1%) cases which had been created on the OCGM and aggregated in June 2014.

Definitions

We defined fraud as those OCGs engaged in current or historic forms of criminality (to a low, medium, or high level) linked to one of over 50 economic crimes recorded via the OCGM process.[2] Following advice from colleagues at the National Crime Agency, other frauds relating to commodity importation, counterfeiting or illegal supply, and organised immigration crime and human trafficking (not for sexual exploitation) were also included within our definition.[3]

Levels of Analysis

Analyses of OCGM data were undertaken at four levels: (i) all OCGs (N = 4824), (ii) those considered to be engaged in high levels of fraud-related criminality (7.2%, n = 347),[4] (iii) groups engaged in low to medium levels of fraud-related criminality (26.9%, n = 1300),[5] and (iv) non-fraud or other OCGs (65.9%, n = 3177). In addition to descriptive statistics relating to all four groups, tests of association were undertaken between (ii), (iii), and (iv) in order to measure differences between them on a range of items collated via the OCGM process.[6]

Results

Intent and Capability

These OCGs were considered to have intent and capability in an average (median) of five different areas (mean=5.25, range=1–11, SD[7] = 2.7, n = 2638). This was most commonly flagged in relation to geographical scope (81.4%), cohesion (69.2%), tactical awareness (61.1%), and cash flow (59.9%). There were fewer OCGs where concerns were identified with regard to their growth potential (48.8%); links to other OCGs (47.3%); resistance/resilience (39.9%); violent capability (38.3%); expertise (35.2%); involvement in multiple enterprises (31.7%); and scope for infiltration, corruption, and subversion (12.5%).

Those groups engaged in high (mean 6.0) and low/medium (5.5) levels of fraud-related criminality were considered to have intent and capability across a wider range of areas than non-fraud OCGs (5.1) ($F(2, 2638) = 11.3$, $p = 0.000$),[8] including in relation to expertise (61.1% vs. 49.0% vs. 26.1%; $\chi^2(2, N = 2638) = 178.2$, $p = 0.000$), infiltration, corruption, and subversion (30.6% vs. 17.7% vs. 8.3%; $\chi^2(2, N = 2638) = 100.1$, $p = 0.000$), involvement in multiple enterprises (48.9% vs. 39.0% vs. 26.6%; $\chi^2(2, N = 2638) = 64.1$, $p = 0.000$), resistance/resilience (58.3% vs. 46.3% vs. 35.1%; $\chi^2(2, N = 2638) = 55.0$, $p = 0.000$), and cash flow (74.4% vs. 65.6% vs. 55.8%; $\chi^2(2, N = 2638) = 38.2$, $p = 0.000$).

By contrast, they were less likely to display violent capability (20.6% vs. 29.7% vs. 44.1%; $\chi^2(2, N = 2638) = 71.6$, $p = 0.000$), have links with other OCGs (44.4% vs. 42.0% vs. 50.0%; $\chi^2(2, N = 2638) = 14.1$, $p = 0.001$), or be considered tactically aware (51.7% vs. 54.8% vs. 65.0%; $\chi^2(2, N = 2638) = 31.5$, $p = 0.000$). There were no differences between fraud and other

OCGs in the extent to which their cohesion was considered to impact upon levels of intent and capability (68.9% vs. 72.2% vs. 67.9%; $\chi^2(2, N = 2638) = 4.7, p = 0.097$).

Similarly, those engaged in high levels of fraud-related criminality—in contrast to those mapped with low/medium levels of criminality in this area—were considered to have intent and capability across a larger number of areas ($t(265.0) = 2.13, p = 0.034$). This was true with regard to infiltration, corruption, and subversion ($\chi^2(1, N = 947) = 14.9, p = 0.000$), growth potential (61.7% vs. 48.0%; $\chi^2(1, N = 947) = 11.0, p = 0.001$), expertise ($\chi^2(1, N = 947) = 8.6, p = 0.003$), resistance/resilience ($\chi^2(1, N = 947) = 8.5, p = 0.004$), involvement in multiple enterprises ($\chi^2(1, N = 947) = 5.9, p = 0.015$), and cash flow ($\chi^2(1, N = 947) = 5.2, p = 0.023$). They were, however, less likely to display violent capability than other fraud groups ($\chi^2(1, N = 947) = 6.1, p = 0.014$).

Quality of Intelligence Around Intent and Capability

From the 11 areas around which the intent and capability of OCGs are measured via the OCGM process, available intelligence was considered to be 'fair' or 'poor' in an average (median) of 10 (mean = 8.7, range = 0–11, $SD = 2.8$, $N = 4824$). This was particularly true with regard to the resistance/resilience of OCGs (92.0%), their potential for infiltration, corruption, and subversion (88.6%), involvement in multiple enterprises (86.3%), cash flow (83.3%), and links to other OCGs (82.0%). There were fewer areas in which the available intelligence on groups engaged in high (mean 7.5) and low/medium (8.2) levels of fraud-related criminality was considered to be 'fair' or 'poor', when compared to non-fraud OCGs (9.0) ($F(2, 4824) = 555.7, p = 0.000$).

The Characteristics of Mapped OCGs

A total of 33,844 individuals (or nominals) were known for 96% of the groups recorded via the OCGM process and used for this analysis. There was an average (median) of five known nominals per OCG (mean = 7.3, range = 1–185, $SD = 9.9$, $n = 4647$). A total of 26,425 male nominals were identified for 88% ($n = 4264$) of mapped OCGs. Where known ($n = 4517$), the ages of mapped OCGs ranged from 17 to 77, with an average (mean) age of 37 years. The main nationality of the OCG was recorded in over four-fifths of cases ($n = 3987$). Two-thirds (68.0%) of these OCGs were flagged as comprising of mainly British nationals.

While there was no difference between fraud-related OCGs and others in terms of the average number of known members (8.0 vs. 7.1 vs. 7.3; ($F(2, 4647) = 109.0$, $p = 0.330$), they had proportionally fewer male nominals (80.4% vs. 83.3% vs. 85.5%; ($F(2, 4264) = 7.7$, $p = 0.000$), were of an older average (mean) age (41.4 vs. 39.1 vs. 36.3; ($F(2, 4517) = 75.1$, $p = 0.000$), and were less likely to be British nationals (49.1% vs. 62.2% vs. 72.8%; $\chi^2(2, N = 3987) = 97.0$, $p = 0.000$).

Compared to those groups engaged in low/medium levels of fraud-related criminality (14.8%) and non-fraud OCGs (9.6%), criminal enterprises mapped as having high levels of fraud-related criminality (30.5%) were significantly more likely to have an international dimension ($\chi^2(2, N = 4824) = 134.1$, $p = 0.000$) and be expanding their enterprises through UK borders (24.2% vs. 10.9% vs. 9.2%; $\chi^2(2, N = 4824) = 74.1$, $p = 0.000$).

An assessment was made about the structure of the OCG for over half of the mapped groups (54.7%). The available data indicated that around one in eight (12.2%) of these OCGs were considered to have a recognised structure, with this being more likely for those groups displaying high levels of fraud-related criminality (18.9%), relative to low/medium criminality fraud-related groups (15.1%) and other OCGs (10.2%) ($\chi^2(2, N = 2638) = 20.0$, $p = 0.000$).

An estimate of group assets was also provided for a similar number of OCGs (52.5%). One in four of these groups (27.0%) had estimated assets in excess of £1 million. Again, this was more likely to be true of those groups mapped with high levels of fraud-related criminality (64.1%), compared to low/medium criminality fraud-related groups (32.3%) and other non-fraud OCGs (16.6%) ($\chi^2(2, N = 2531) = 269.4$, $p = 0.000$).

Mapped OCGs were considered to impact upon these locations in a variety of ways: by nominals living there (67.3%), through the groups' realisation of gain from criminal activity in these areas (44.8%), through victims of OCG activity being resident there (35.7%), and by key criminal infrastructure being situated in these locations (21.7%). Compared to other OCGs, those involved in fraud-related activities were more likely to impact on communities through realisation of gain in these locations (47.6% vs. 55.7% vs. 40.1%; $\chi^2(2, N = 4789) = 92.0$, $p = 0.000$), by having victims of their criminal activity resident there (28.8% vs. 39.5% vs. 35.0%; $\chi^2(2, N = 4789) = 15.9$, $p = 0.000$), and by having both key criminal infrastructure (33.1% vs. 24.8% vs. 19.2%; $\chi^2(2, N = 4789) = 46.1$, $p = 0.000$) and nominals living there (64.8% vs. 72.7% vs. 65.4%; $\chi^2(2, N = 4789) = 23.3$, $p = 0.000$).

Relative to other fraud-related OCGs, however, those identified as having a high level of criminality in this area were less likely to impact on communities through having victims of their criminal activity residing there ($\chi^2(1, N = 1639) = 13.3, p = 0.000$), by having key criminal infrastructure ($\chi^2(1, N = 1639) = 9.6, p = 0.002$) or nominals living within these communities ($\chi^2(1, N = 1639) = 8.2, p = 0.004$), or as a consequence of realising the potential gains in these locations ($\chi^2(2, N = 1639) = 7.4, p = 0.007$).

Just under one-third (31.7%) of the mapped OCGs had known links to other criminal enterprises (e.g. through the sharing of nominals, companies, associates, collaboration, or rivalry). There were known links between 1926 OCGs, with each group associated with an average (median) of one other criminal enterprise (mean = 1.7, range = 1–14, $SD = 1.4$, $n = 1168$).

Nature and Extent of Harm

When compared to other criminal enterprises, fraud-related OCGs were significantly more likely to be assessed via the mapping process as having:

- An exceptional level of criminality (e.g. operating at a scale and frequency that was deemed to exceed typical thresholds) (35.3% vs. 10.4% vs. 5.3%; $\chi^2(2, N = 4450) = 332.4, p = 0.000$)
- A pivotal role in enabling substantial criminality among other OCGs (20.2% vs. 6.3% vs. 3.2%; $\chi^2(2, N = 4450) = 172.7, p = 0.000$)
- Primary or secondary criminal activities not being assessed using the current OCGM framework (9.4% vs. 4.4% vs. 2.0%; $\chi^2(2, N = 4450) = 58.8, p = 0.000$)
- Political/reputational damage arising from their activities (e.g. linked to any negative opinion that the community may have of law enforcement or other public body in relation to their response to the OCG's activities) (6.6% vs. 1.8% vs. 0.5%; $\chi^2(2, N = 2854) = 56.6, p = 0.000$)
- Impact upon a community to an exceptional level, far exceeding that normally associated with their type of criminality (11.2% vs. 9.2% vs. 6.4%; $\chi^2(2, N = 4450) = 15.1, p = 0.000$)

These differences were largely driven by those engaged in high levels of fraud-related criminality. In contrast to other fraud-related groups, these OCGs were mapped as having an exceptional level of criminality ($\chi^2(2, N = 1571) = 123.1, p = 0.000$), a pivotal role to play in enabling substantial criminality among other groups ($\chi^2(1, N = 1571) = 60.1, p = 0.000$), potential for considerable political/reputational damage arising from their offending ($\chi^2(1, N = 1139) = 16.3, p = 0.000$), and key elements of their criminal activities unassessed using the current mapping framework ($\chi^2(1, N = 1571) = 12.8, p = 0.000$).

Specialist Roles and Links to Business
Three-quarters (75.8%) of these OCGs had at least one known specialist role within the enterprise, with an average (median) of two identified (mean = 2.8, range = 0–16, $SD = 1.9$, $n = 3524$). By contrast only one in eight (11.6%) OCGs had details of a regulated occupation within the group recorded on OCGM. Fraud-related OCGs were more likely to have had a regulated occupation reported (26.6% vs. 17.2% vs. 7.8%; $\chi^2(2, N = 4647) = 152.5, p = 0.000$), as well as a specialist role identified (82.9% vs. 82.3% vs. 72.5%; $\chi^2(2, N = 4647) = 55.9, p = 0.000$), and have more of these specialist roles present within their groups (3.5 vs. 3.1 vs. 2.6; ($F(2, 3524) = 48.9, p = 0.000$). Regulated occupations were more likely to be reported within those groups engaged in high levels of fraud-related criminality, in contrast to other fraud groups ($\chi^2(1, N = 1560) = 14.8, p = 0.000$), and they had more specialist roles present within them ($p = 0.036$).

Over a third (36.6%) of the OCGs had links—current and historic—to a total of 7065 companies. These groups had links with an average (median) of two companies (mean = 4.0, range = 1–184, $SD = 7.2$, $n = 1765$) in different capacities. These ranged from owning the company (73.7%), managing (11.8%) or operating from it (11.2%), working there (9.6%), investing in it (8.9%), or performing some other (unspecified) role (33.5%). Available intelligence data via OCGM indicated that some of these were considered legitimate businesses complicit in laundering (17.5%), facilitating serious crime (15.2%), or serving as a front to import/export goods (6.7%). There were far fewer legitimate companies flagged as being non-complicit in laundering (2.2%).

Mapped OCGs engaged in fraud had links with more companies (8.5 vs. 4.7 vs. 2.6; ($F(2, 1765) = 57.9, p = 0.000$) and were more likely to be linked to them in the capacity of an owner (80.4% vs. 77.4% vs. 69.7%; $\chi^2(2, N = 1706) = 16.1, p = 0.000$), manager (17.9% vs. 13.5% vs. 9.4%; $\chi^2(2, N = 1706) = 12.8, p = 0.002$), or operative (13.4% vs. 14.2% vs. 8.5%; $\chi^2(2, N = 1706) = 13.3, p = 0.001$). There were no differences in the extent to which these groups were linked to these companies as investors (9.5% vs. 8.8% vs. 8.7%; $\chi^2(2, N = 1706) = 0.1, p = 0.948$) or in some other (unspecified) way (36.9% vs. 33.1% vs. 33.1%; $\chi^2(2, N = 1706) = 1.0, p = 0.606$). Compared to other OCGs, the legitimate companies to which fraud-related criminal enterprises were linked were also significantly more likely to be complicit in facilitating serious crime (27.1% vs. 17.8% vs. 11.1%; $\chi^2(2, N = 1764) = 35.2, p = 0.000$), laundering (31.5% vs. 19.3% vs. 13.5%; $\chi^2(2, N = 1764) = 36.3, p = 0.000$), and acting as a front to import/export goods (23.8% vs. 5.4% vs. 4.2%; $\chi^2(2, N = 1764) = 95.0, p = 0.000$).

Those engaged in high levels of fraud-related activity had links with more companies than other (low/medium criminality) fraud OCGs ($t(842) = 4.7, p = 0.000$), but with no significant differences between them in the way in which they were linked to these companies. Compared to other fraud OCGs, the legitimate businesses to which these high criminality fraud groups had links were significantly more likely to be acting as a front to import/export goods ($\chi^2(1, N = 856) = 49.8, p = 0.000$), be complicit in laundering ($\chi^2(1, N = 858) = 8.8, p = 0.003$), and facilitating serious crime ($\chi^2(1, N = 858) = 5.2, p = 0.023$).

One in five (21.0%) of the mapped OCGs had a link with an identifiable business sector. Where known, most OCGs had a link with only one business sector (mean = 1.7, median 1, range = 1–8, $SD = 1.1$, $n = 1011$). As illustrated in Fig. A1, one in four had reported links to the vehicle/transport industry (24.9%), with fewer known to be associated with the catering (16.9%) and service sectors (16.1%), or professional (14.8%) and property services (12.6%). Many (43.3%) though operated within another (unspecified) sector.

OCGs engaged in fraud-related activities were more likely to have an identifiable link with business (40.9% vs. 30.7% vs. 14.8%; $\chi^2(2, N = 4824) = 230.7, p = 0.000$), in particular professional services (21.6% vs. 20.1% vs. 7.0%; $\chi^2(2, N = 1011) = 45.5, p = 0.000$) and other (unspecified) sectors (62.7% vs. 47.1% vs. 34.3%; $\chi^2(2, N = 1011) = 39.7, p = 0.000$). Conversely, they were less likely to have links with the catering (9.2% vs. 14.8% vs. 21.1%; $\chi^2(2, N = 1011) = 13.1, p = 0.001$) and health/beauty sectors (4.2% vs. 7.0% vs. 12.1%; $\chi^2(2, N = 1011) = 11.5, p = 0.003$). There were no significant differences between fraud-related OCGs and others in the number of different business sectors they were known to be linked to ($F(2, 1011) = 1.6, p = 0.203$). By contrast, those engaged in high levels of fraud-related criminality were significantly more likely to be linked with other (unspecified) business sectors than other fraud-related OCGs ($\chi^2(1, N = 541) = 10.2, p = 0.001$), but less likely to have links with the environmental sector ($\chi^2(1, N = 541) = 4.6, p = 0.033$).

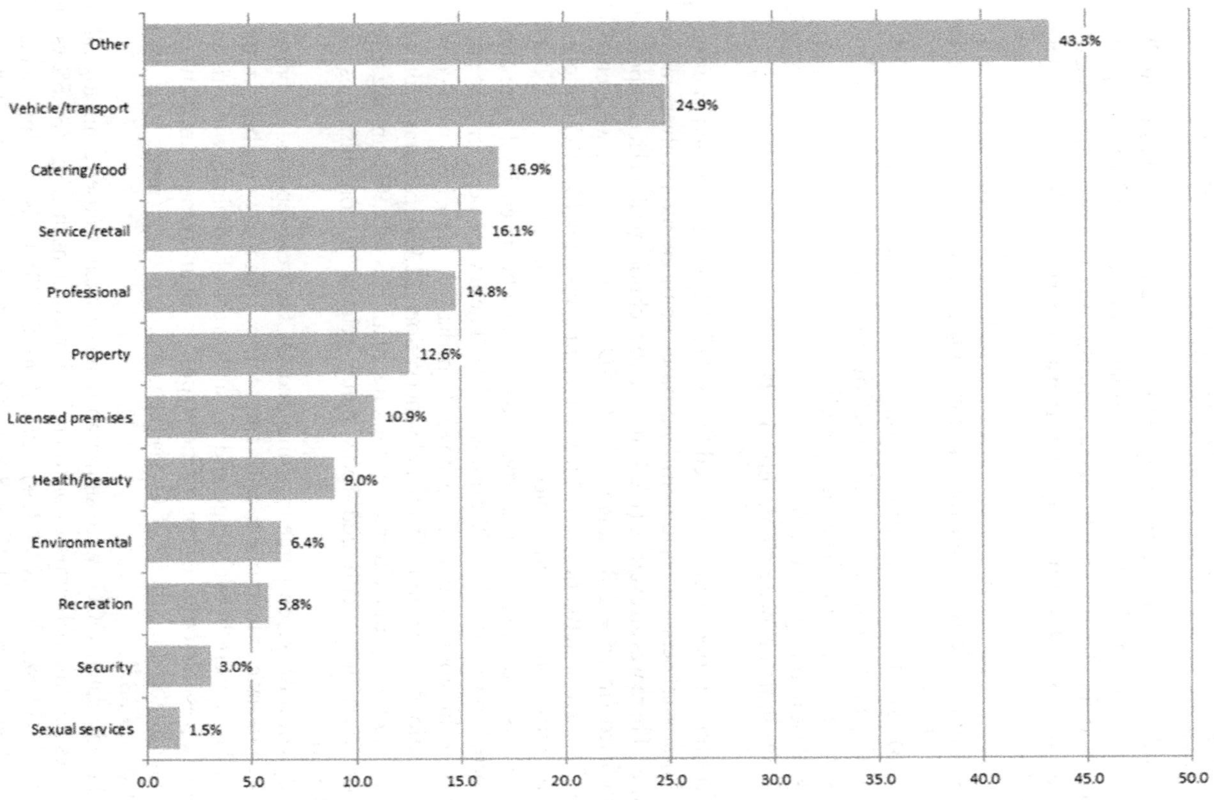

Fig. A1 Known OCG links to business sectors ($N = 1011$)

Extent to Which Criminality Is Considered to Be Internet/Technology Enabled[9]

Around one in seven (13.9%) mapped OCGs were identified as using the Internet as an enabler. The average (median) number of different purposes identified for the Internet being used in this way was two (mean = 2.3, range = 1–6, *SD* = 1.6, *n* = 669). It was reportedly adopted by these OCGs to:

- Communicate within their group and/or other criminal networks (71.2%)
- Market, buy, or sell criminal goods and services (42.8%)
- Organise the group's criminal activity (48.1%)
- Communicate with victims (26.6%)
- Research targets (19.7%)
- Promote or incite criminality (18.2%)

A similar proportion of mapped OCGs (17.4%) were identified as using technological services for criminal purposes or to enable involvement in crime. There was an average (median) of two technological services reportedly used (mean = 2.3, range = 1–19, *SD* = 1.9, *n* = 841), with email (60.2%), social networks (44.1%), and instant messaging (27.1%) the platforms most commonly identified.

Details of the number and type of technology being enabled were also reported to OCGM for 179 groups (3.7%). There were between one and seven technologies reported (mean=1.7, median=1, *SD* = 1.3), with communications encryption (31.3%), file encryption (22.9%), cameras (stills or video) (18.4%), and alternative banking platforms (22.9%) among the most frequently mentioned tools being relayed by organisations to OCGM.

By contrast, seven percent of mapped OCGs were reported as being known to have at least one specific Internet- or technology-enabled crime type. There were between one and six such areas of criminality identified (from a possible range of ten offence types), with an average (median) of two highlighted for these OCGs via the mapping process (mean = 1.8, *SD* = 1.0, *n* = 333).

Fraud-related OCGs were significantly more likely to use technological services for criminal purposes or to enable involvement in crime (39.5% vs. 25.8% vs. 11.6%; $\chi^2(2, N = 4824) = 254.7, p = 0.000$), to use the Internet as an enabler (32.6% vs. 21.4% vs. 8.8%; $\chi^2(2, N = 4824) = 232.7, p = 0.000$), and to be engaged in a specific Internet- or technology-enabled crime type (16.4% vs. 13.8% vs. 3.0%; $\chi^2(2, N = 4824) = 221.0, p = 0.000$). In contrast to other fraud OCGs, those involved in a high level of fraud-related criminality were more likely to exploit technological services for criminal purposes or to facilitate involvement in crime ($\chi^2(1, N = 1647) = 25.2, p = 0.000$), and use the Internet as an enabler ($\chi^2(1, N = 1647) = 18.9, p = 0.000$).

What Factors Predict Involvement in a High Level of Fraud-Related Criminality?[10]

Univariate and multiple logistic regression analyses were used to explore which factors recorded via the OCGM process best predicted involvement in a high level of organised fraud-related criminality. The independent predictor variables examined aspects of intent and capability, characteristics of the OCG, level of assessed harm, the presence of specialist roles, links to companies, and use of technology. These results are set out in Tables A1 and A2.

These showed that OCGs involved in a high level of fraud-related criminality, and mapped via the OCGM process, were five times more likely than others to have estimated assets in excess of £1 million. They were almost three times more likely to have been assessed as generating significant political/reputational damage arising from their activities. Compared to other OCGs, those criminal enterprises engaged in a high level of fraud-related criminality were also twice as likely to have:

- An international dimension
- Used technological services for criminal purposes
- A regulated occupation within their ranks
- An identifiable link with the business sector

The odds of being identified as playing a pivotal role in enabling substantial criminality among other OCGs were 93% higher among those engaged in a high level of fraud-related criminality. Furthermore, the odds of involvement in an additional area of criminality (besides fraud) were 25% higher for these groups, relative to other OCGs. By contrast, the odds of these criminal enterprises being assessed via the OCGM process as being mainly British was 39% lower for those OCGs engaged in high levels of fraud-related criminality. They were also 40% less likely to be involved in multiple enterprises.

Table A1 Predictors of involvement in a high level of fraud-related criminality—multivariate regression ($N = 4824$)

Independent variables	*Multivariate regression*[a]					
	B	*SE*	χ^2	*p*	*Exp (B)*	*95 CI (of Exp B)*
Has estimated assets of over £1 m	1.634	0.243	45.04	0.000	5.124	3.180–8.258
Political/reputational damage arising from their activities	0.990	0.505	3.85	0.050	2.691	1.001–7.239
Has an international dimension	0.866	0.245	12.47	0.000	2.377	1.470–3.844
Uses technological services for criminal purposes	0.838	0.233	12.97	0.000	2.311	1.465–3.647
Details of a regulated occupation within the OCG recorded	0.719	0.230	9.72	0.002	2.051	1.306–3.223
Primary or secondary criminal activities not assessed	0.690	0.416	2.75	0.097	1.994	0.882–4.507
Has an identifiable link with the business sector	0.687	0.254	7.30	0.007	1.989	1.208–3.273
Plays a pivotal role in enabling substantial criminality among other OCGs	0.659	0.292	5.10	0.024	1.933	1.091–3.427
Number of areas of criminality OCG known to be involved in (max 10)	0.220	0.077	8.23	0.004	1.246	1.072–1.447
Number of companies OCG has a known link to (includes current and historic)	0.035	0.015	5.08	0.024	1.035	1.005–1.067
OCG main nationality is British	−0.496	0.240	4.28	0.039	0.609	0.381–0.974
Involvement in multiple enterprises	−0.516	0.241	4.58	0.032	0.597	0.372–0.957
Constant	−4.692	0.363	166.97	0.000	0.009	

[a]Hosmer and Lemeshow test: $\chi^2(8) = 4.3$, $p = 0.828$, $R^2 = 0.400$

Table A2 Predictors of involvement in a high level of fraud-related criminality—univariate relationships ($N = 4824$)

Independent variables	*Univariate regression*					
	B	*SE*	χ^2	*p*	*Exp (B)*	*95 CI (of Exp B)*
Intent and capability: expertise	1.148	0.159	52.2	0.000	3.151	2.308–4.301
Infiltration, corruption, and subversion	1.247	0.174	51.4	0.000	3.479	2.474–4.892
Involvement in multiple enterprises	0.782	0.155	25.342	0.000	2.187	1.612–2.965
Resistance/resilience	0.802	0.157	26.173	0.000	2.230	1.640–3.032
Cash flow	0.712	0.176	16.43	0.000	2.039	1.445–2.877
OCG characteristics: is mainly British	−0.870	0.118	54.6	0.000	0.419	0.332–0.528
Has an international dimension	1.257	0.126	99.7	0.000	3.514	2.746–4.498
Has a recognised structure	0.558	0.200	7.76	0.005	1.748	1.180–2.589
Has estimated assets of over £1 m	1.802	0.139	168.3	0.000	6.059	4.615–7.954
Number of areas of criminality OCG known to be involved in (max 10)	0.475	0.036	177.0	0.000	1.608	1.499–1.724
Harm: a pivotal role in enabling substantial criminality among other OCGs	1.768	0.158	125.9	0.000	5.859	4.303–7.979
Primary or secondary criminal activities not assessed	1.308	0.212	38.16	0.000	3.697	2.442–5.597
Political/reputational damage arising from their activities	1.991	0.328	36.95	0.000	7.326	3.86–13.92
Impacts upon a community to an exceptional level	0.479	0.185	6.72	0.010	1.614	1.124–2.317

(*continued*)

Table A2 (continued)

Independent variables	*Univariate regression*					
	B	*SE*	χ^2	*p*	*Exp (B)*	*95 CI (of Exp B)*
Specialist roles, links to companies, and use of technology: details of a regulated occupation within the OCG recorded	1.130	0.135	70.39	0.000	3.094	2.377–4.029
Has at least one specialist role	0.462	0.151	9.367	0.002	1.587	1.181–2.134
Number of companies OCG has a known link to (includes current and historic)	0.084	0.010	70.01	0.000	1.088	1.067–1.110
Has an identifiable link with the business sector	1.056	0.116	83.60	0.000	2.876	2.293–3.607
Uses technological services for criminal purposes	1.252	0.117	113.98	0.000	3.496	2.779–4.400
Any areas of criminality flagged on OCGM as Internet/ technology enabled	1.096	0.158	48.32	0.000	2.992	2.196–4.075

Glossary

ATM (cash machine) fraud	ATM fraud occurs when a credit or debit card, or the card's information, is taken by fraudsters when a member of the public uses a cash machine or ATM. http://www.actionfraud.police.uk/fraud-az-cash-point-fraud
Courier fraud	Courier fraud occurs when a victim is called on the telephone by an individual pretending to be from their bank or building society. The victim is persuaded to part with their credit/debit card details over the phone. The offender arranges for a courier to pick up the victim's card stating that it is needed as evidence or that it needs to be destroyed. In reality, the card is collected by the offenders who, following the phone call, have all the information needed to de-fraud the victim's bank account. http://www.actionfraud.police.uk/fraud-az-courier-scam
Debit and credit card fraud	When personal information is stolen from a victim's debit, credit or store card, or the card itself is stolen. The purpose of this is to enable the offender to steal money from the victim's account or use the card)s) to buy items in the victim's name. http://www.actionfraud.police.uk/fraud-az-store-card-fraud
Distribution fraud	Distribution fraud occurs when a legitimate company from overseas (usually Europe) delivers products to the UK, but does not receive payment for the goods or the cost of shipping. Fraudsters profess to be from a well-known company or business to make their order look authentic. The goods are sold to a third person/company at 100% profit. http://www.actionfraud.police.uk/fraud-az-edf

T. May, B. Bhardwa, *Organised Crime Groups involved in Fraud*,
Crime Prevention and Security Management,
https://doi.org/10.1007/978-3-319-69401-6

Employee fraud Internal or employee frauds are committed when employees abuse their privileged position to commit fraud against their employer. Internal frauds can include payment fraud, procurement fraud, travel and subsistence fraud, personnel management fraud, exploiting assets and information fraud, and receipt fraud.
http://www.actionfraud.police.uk/fraud-az-employee-fraud

False accounting False accounting fraud occurs when company's assets are overstated or liabilities are understated to make a business appear financially stronger than it really is. False accounting fraud involves an employee or an organisation altering, destroying, or defacing an account or presenting accounts from an individual or an organisation so they don't reflect their true value or the financial activities of that company. False accounting can take place for a number of reasons: to obtain additional financing from a bank, to report unrealistic profits, to inflate the share price, to hide losses, to attract customers by appearing to be more successful than one is, to achieve a performance-related bonus, and to cover up theft.
http://www.actionfraud.police.uk/fraud-protection/false-accounting-fraud

Insolvency fraud Insolvency fraud occurs when a company attempts to do business whilst insolvent, such as applying for credit or trading while suspended or disqualified, or reforms as a phoenix company to avoid paying creditors.
http://www.actionfraud.police.uk/fraud-az-insolvency-related-fraud

Insurance fraud Insurance-related frauds occur when a false claim is made to an insurance company. A false insurance claim occurs when an individual claims to have financially lost more than they have or they make more than one claim for the same item/incident. Alternatively, a person might deliberately destroy the asset they are claiming insurance for.
Insurance fraud also occurs when an individual provides false information to an insurance company in an attempt to purchase insurance cover on more favourable terms or deliberately under-insuring to reduce the premium. This type of insurance fraud includes motor vehicle, commercial, household, and other personal insurance claims.
http://www.actionfraud.police.uk/fraud-az-insurance-fraud

Investment fraud When a member of the public receives a cold telephone call from a fake broker pretending to offer the victim the opportunity to invest in a variety of schemes or products that are either worthless or don't exist. This type of fraud is also referred to as share sale fraud, hedge fund fraud, land banking fraud, or bond fraud. The majority of investment frauds are run out of offices known as 'boiler rooms'.
http://www.actionfraud.police.uk/fraud-az-investment-fraud

Making or supplying articles for the use of fraud	Supplying articles for the purpose of fraud involves an offender making, adapting, supplying, or offering to supply any article for use in the course of or in connection with fraud.
Money laundering and movement of money	The movement of money which relates to fraud occurs when the proceeds of crime from fraud, or money needed to fund fraudulent activity, is moved. Money could be moved by virtual payment systems, which can obscure the payment trail for online criminal activities or when the offenders buy stolen credit card or bank account details. The offenders may also use electronic money exchangers and international transfer agents to move funds between different systems. Hawala banking might be used for the non-electric transfer of funds. Offenders may also use prepaid debit or credit cards or other prepaid cards and vouchers. http://www.actionfraud.police.uk/fraud-az-money-movement
Mortgage fraud	Mortgage fraud is when a mortgage, or multiple mortgages, is obtained fraudulently. Mortgage fraud usually involves individual(s) or organised criminal groups and at least one corrupt associate, such as an accountant, solicitor, or surveyor. Mortgage fraud can include over-valuing properties, overstating a salary or income, hijacking genuine conveyancing processes, taking out mortgages in the name of unsuspecting individuals or stealing the identity of those who are deceased, taking out a number of mortgages with different lenders on one address by manipulating Land Registry data, and changing title deeds without an owner's knowledge to allow the sale of a property. http://www.actionfraud.police.uk/fraud-az-mortgage-fraud
Romance fraud	Romance fraud occurs when a victim believes they have met the perfect partner through an online dating website or app; however, the offender is using a fake profile to form a relationship with the victim. The offender uses the site to gain a victim's trust and to ask for money or enough personal information to steal the victim's identity. http://www.actionfraud.police.uk/fraud_protection/dating_fraud
Customs and revenue fraud	Tax fraud involves the theft of taxes due to HMRC or tax credits paid out by HMRC. Tax fraud includes tax evasion, where an individual or company avoids their tax liability by deliberately failing to declare their income, or by falsifying expenses. It also includes smuggling goods that are liable to excise duty, customs duty, or VAT. Tax theft can happen when a person claims amounts that are not due. Tax fraud also happens when VAT is charged on a product, but that tax is not paid to the government and is instead stolen by the fraudster. This is known as missing trader intra-community fraud (MTIC) or carousel fraud. http://www.actionfraud.police.uk/fraud-az-tax-fraud

References

Action Fraud. (2017). What Is Fraud and Cyber Crime? *Action Fraud* [Online]. Available at: http://www.actionfraud.police.uk/what-is-fraud. Accessed 10 May 2017.

Albanese, J. (2005). Fraud: The Characteristic Crime of the 21st Century. *Trends in Organized Crime, 8*(4), 6–14.

Button, M. (2011). Fraud Investigation and the 'Flawed Architecture' of Counter Fraud Entities in the United Kingdom. *International Journal of Law, Crime and Justice, 39*, 249–265.

Button, M. and Tunley, M. (2015). Explaining Fraud Deviancy Attenuation in the United Kingdom. *Crime, Law and Social Change, 63*(1–2), 49–64.

Button, M. Johnston, L., Frimpong, K., and Smith, G. (2007). New Directions in Policing Fraud: The Emergence of the Counter Fraud Specialist in the United Kingdom. *International Journal of the Sociology of Law, 35*, 192–208.

Button, M. Blackbourn, D., and Tunley, M. (2015). 'The Not So Thin Blue Line After All?' Investigative Resources Dedicated to Fighting Fraud/Economic Crime in the United Kingdom. *Policing, 9*(2), 129–142.

Button, M. Shepherd, D., Blackbourn, D., and Tunley, M. (2016). Annual Fraud Indicator 2016. *Experian, PKF Littlejohn and the University of Portsmouth's Centre for Counter Fraud Studies.* Available at http://www.port.ac.uk/media/contacts-and-departments/icjs/ccfs/Annual-Fraud-Indicator-2016.pdf

Cifas. (2016). *Fraudscape 2016.* London: Cifas.

T. May, B. Bhardwa, *Organised Crime Groups involved in Fraud*, Crime Prevention and Security Management, https://doi.org/10.1007/978-3-319-69401-6

City of London Police. (2015). *National Policing Fraud Strategy*. Draft Prepared by the National Police Coordinator for Economic Crime January 2015. London: City of London Police. Available at http://democracy.cityoflondon.gov.uk/documents/s50106/Pol_24-15_Appendix_1_Draft%20Police%20Fraud%20Strategy%20v%202.2.pdf. Accessed 12 May 2017.

Cram, F. (2013). Understanding the Proceeds of Crime Act 2002: Cash Seizure and Frontline Policing. *The Howard Journal of Criminal Justice, 52*(2), 121–131.

Cressey, D. R. (1953). *Other People's Money*. Glencoe: The Free Press.

Doig, A. and Levi, M. (2013). A Case of Arrested Development? Delivering the UK National Fraud Strategy Within Competing Policing Policy Priorities. *Public Money & Management, 33*(2), 145–152.

Doig, A., Johnson, S., and Levi, M. (2001). New Public Management, Old Populism and the Policing of Fraud. *Public Policy and Administration, 16*, 9.

Dorn, N., Murji, K., and South, N. (1992). *Traffickers: Drug Markets and Law Enforcement*. London: Routledge.

Edwards, A. (2004). Understanding Organised Crime. *Criminal Justice Matters, 55*(1), 30–31.

Edwards, A. and Levi, M. (2008). Researching the Organization of Serious Crimes. *Criminology and Criminal Justice, 8*(4), 363–388.

Europol. (2017a). EU Serious and Organised Crime Threat Assessment: Crime in the Age of Technology. *Europol* [Online]. Available at https://www.europol.europa.eu/newsroom/news/crime-in-age-of-technology-%E2%80%93-europol%E2%80%99s-serious-and-organised-crime-threat-assessment-2017. Accessed 26 Apr 2017.

Europol. (2017b). Economic Crime. *Europol* [Online]. Available at https://www.europol.europa.eu/crime-areas-and-trends/crime-areas/economic-crime. Accessed 26 Apr 2017.

Felson, M. (2006). *The Ecosystem for Organized Crime*. Helsinki: European Institute for Crime Prevention and Control, affiliated with the United Nations.

Financial Times. (2017). Global Financial Crisis. *Financial Times* [Online]. Available at: https://www.ft.com/global-financial-crisis. Accessed 26 Apr 2017.

Finckenauer, J. O. (2005). Problems of Definition: What Is Organized Crime? *Trends in Organized Crime, 8*, 63–83.

Francis, B., Humphreys, L., Kirby, S., and Soothill, K. (2013). *Understanding Criminal Careers in Organised Crime* (Research Report 74). London: Home Office.

Fraud Advisory Panel. (2016). *The Fraud Review—Ten Years On* [Online]. Available at: https://www.fraudadvisorypanel.org/wp-content/uploads/2016/06/The-Fraud-Review-Ten-Years-On-WEB.pdf. Accessed 5 Apr 2017.

Gannon, R. and Doig, A. (2010). Ducking the Answer? Fraud Strategies and Police Resources. *Policing and Society, 20*(1), 39–60.

Garner, S., Crocker, R., Skidmore, M., Webb, S., Graham, J., and Gill, M. (2016). *Reducing the Impact of Serious Organised Crime in Local Communities: Organised Fraud in Local Communities* (Briefing 1). Perpetuity Research and the Police Foundation. http://www.police-foundation.org.uk/uploads/holding/projects/org_fraud_in_local_communities_final.pdf

Gee, J. and Button, M. (2013). *The Financial Cost of Fraud Report 2013*. London/Portsmouth: BDO and Centre for Counter Fraud Studies.

Gill, M. (2005). *Learning from Fraudsters*. London: Protiviti Ltd.

Gill, M., and Randall, A. (2015). *Insurance Fraudsters*. Kent: Perpetuity Research and Consultancy International (PRCI) Ltd.

Grabosky, P. (2013). Organised Crime and the Internet: Implications for National Security. *The RUSI Journal, 158*(5), 18–25.

Harfield, C. (2008). The Organization of 'Organized Crime Policing' and Its International Context. *Criminology & Criminal Justice, 8*(4), 483–507.

HM Government. (2006). *Fraud Review: Final Report*. London: Home Office.

HMIC. (2015). Regional Organised Crime Units: A Review of Capability and Effectiveness. *Her Majesty's Inspectorate of Constabulary* [Online]. Available at: https://www.justiceinspectorates.gov.uk/hmic/wp-content/uploads/regional-organised-crime-units.pdf. Accessed 10 May 2017.

Hobbs, D. (1998). Going Down the Glocal: The Local Context of Organised Crime. *The Howard Journal of Criminal Justice, 37*(4), 407–422.

Hobbs, D. (2013). *Lush Life: Constructing Organized Crime in the UK*. Oxford: Oxford University Press.

Home Office. (2009). *Extending Our Reach: A Comprehensive Approach to Tackling Organised Crime*. London: The Stationery Office.

Home Office. (2011). *Local to Global: Reducing the Risk from Organised Crime*. London: Home Office.

Home Office. (2012). *The Strategic Policing Requirement*. London: Home Office.

Home Office. (2013). *Serious and Organised Crime Strategy*. London: Home Office.

Home Office. (2017). Home Office Counting Rules for Recorded Crime 2017. *Home Office* [Online]. Available at: https://www.gov.uk/government/uploads/system/uploads/attachment_data/file/602811/count-fraud-apr-2017.pdf. Accessed 10 May 2017.

Kirby, S. and Penna, S. (2010). Policing Mobile Criminality: Towards a Situational Crime Prevention Approach to Organised Crime. In K. Bullock, R. V. Clarke, & N. Tilley (Eds.), *Situational Prevention of Organised Crimes*. Cullompton: Willan.

Kirby, S., Francis, B., Humphreys, L., and Soothill, K. (2016). Using the UK General Offender Database as a Means to Measure and Analyse Organized Crime. *Policing: An International Journal of Police Strategies & Management, 39*(1), 78–94.

Kleemans, E. R. (2013). Organized Crime and the Visible Hand: A Theoretical Critique on the Economic Analysis of Organized Crime. *Criminology and Criminal Justice, 13*, 615.

Kleemans, E. R. and De Poot, C. J. (2008). Criminal Careers in Organized Crime and Social Opportunity Structure. *European Journal of Criminology, 5*(1), 69–98.

Kleemans, E. and van de Bunt, H. (2008). Organised Crime, Occupations and Opportunity. *Global Crime, 9*(3), 185–197.

KPMG. (2017, January 24). Value of UK Fraud Breaks £1 Billion Barrier for the First Time in Five Years. *KPMG* [Online]. Available at: https://home.kpmg.com/uk/en/home/insights/2017/01/uk-fraud-value-reaches-1bn-first-time-five-years.html. Accessed 10 May 2017.

Lavorgna, A., Lombardo, R., and Sergi, A. (2013). Organized Crime in Three Regions: Comparing the Veneto, Liverpool, and Chicago. *Trends in Organized Crime, 16*, 265–285.

Le, V. (2012). Organised Crime Typologies: Structure, Activities and Conditions. *International Journal of Criminology and Sociology, 1*, 121–131.

Levi, M. (2008). Organized Fraud and Organizing Frauds: Unpacking Research on Networks and Organization. *Criminology and Criminal Justice, 8*(4), 389–419.

Levi, M. (2010). Hitting the Suite Spot: Sentencing Frauds. *Journal of Financial Crime, 17*(1), 116–132.

Levi, M. (2012). The Organization of Serious Crimes for Gain. In M. Maguire, R. Morgan, & R. Reiner (Eds.), *The Oxford Handbook of Criminology*. Oxford: Oxford University Press.

Levi, M. (2013) Policing Organised Crime: Changing Landscape, Changing Practice. In *Police Foundation Annual Conference 2013*.

Levi, M. and Burrows, J. (2008). Measuring the Impact of Fraud in the UK: A Conceptual and Empirical Journey. *British Journal of Criminology, 48*(3), 293–318.

Levi, M., Doig, A., Gundur, R., Wall, D., & Williams, M. (2015, October). *The Implications of Economic Cybercrime for Policing* (Research Report). London: City of London Corporation.

McDonough, B., Silverstone, D., and Young, T. (Eds.). (2014). *Social Problems in the UK: An Introduction*. London: Routledge.

Mills, H., Skodbo, S., and Blyth, P. (2013). *Understanding Organised Crime: Estimating the Scale and the Social and Economic Costs* (Research Report 73). London: Home Office.

Morselli, C., Turcotte, M., and Tenti, V. (2011). The Mobility of Criminal Groups. *Global Crime, 12*(3), 165–188.

National Fraud Authority. (2011). *Fighting Fraud Together: The Strategic Plan to Reduce Fraud*. London: Home Office.

National Fraud Authority. (2013a). *Annual Fraud Indicator*. https://www.gov.uk/government/uploads/system/uploads/attachment_data/file/206552/nfa-annual-fraud-indicator-2013.pdf

National Fraud Authority. (2013b). *Fighting Fraud Together, Quarterly Update—April 2013*. London: Home Office.

NCA. (2013). National Crime Agency Goes Live. *NCA* [Online]. Available at: http://www.nationalcrimeagency.gov.uk/news/193-nca-launch-article. Accessed 10 May 2017.

NCA. (2014). *National Crime Agency Annual Report and Accounts 2013/14*. National Crime Agency.

NCA. (2015). *National Strategic Assessment of Serious and Organised Crime 2015*. National Crime Agency.

NCA. (2016a). *National Strategic Assessment of Serious and Organised Crime 2016*. National Crime Agency.

NCA. (2016b). Strategic Cyber Industry Group: Cyber Crime Assessment 2016. *Need for a Stronger Law Enforcement and Business Partnership to Fight Cyber Crime 2016*. National Crime Agency.

ONS. (2016a). Overview of Fraud Statistics: Year Ending Mar 2016. *Office of National Statistics* [Online]. Available at: https://www.ons.gov.uk/peoplepopulationandcommunity/crimeandjustice/articles/overviewoffraudstatistics/yearendingmarch2016. Accessed 26 Apr 2017.

ONS. (2016b). Crime in England and Wales: Year Ending Sept 2016 [Online]. Available at: https://www.ons.gov.uk/peoplepopulationandcommunity/crimeandjustice. Accessed 26 Apr 2017.

Paoli, L. (2003). The Informal Economy and Organized Crime. In J. Shapland, H. Albrecht, J. Ditton, & T. Godefroy (Eds.), *The Informal Economy: Threat and Opportunity in the City* (pp. 133–172). Freiburg: Edition iuscrim.

Penna, S. and Kirby, S. (2013). Bridge Over the River Crime: Mobility and the Policing of Organised Crime. *Mobilities, 8*(4), 487–505.

Reuter, P. (1983). *Disorganised Crime: Illegal Markets and the Mafia—The Economics of the Visible Hand*. Cambridge, MA: MIT Press.

Rudd, A. (2016). *Home Secretary's Speech to the FCA's Financial Crime Conference* [Online]. Available at: https://www.gov.uk/government/speeches/home-secretarys-speech-to-the-fcas-financial-crime-conference. Accessed 12 May 2017.

Savona, E. U. and Riccardi, M. (2015). *From Illegal Markets to Legitimate Businesses: The Portfolio of Organised Crime in Europe*. Trento: Transcrime–Università degli Studi di Trento.

Schuchter, A., & Levi, M. (2013). The Fraud Triangle Revisited. *Security Journal*. https://doi.org/10.1057/sj.2013.1. Available online at: http://www.palgrave-journals.com.ezproxy.lib.bbk.ac.uk/sj/journal/vaop/ncurrent/pdf/sj20131a.pdf

Serious Fraud Office (SFO). (2017). *About Us SFO* [Online]. Available at: https://www.sfo.gov.uk/about-us/. Accessed 10 May 2017.

Serious Fraud Office (SFO). *Annual Report and Accounts 2012–13*. Norwich/London: The Stationery Office. http://www.sfo.gov.uk/media/256255/30597%20hc%209.pdf

Silverstone, D. (2014). Organised Crime and It's Policing. In S. Isaacs, D. Blundell, A. Foley, N. Ginsburg, B. McDonough, D. Silverstone, & T. Young (Eds.), *Social Problems in the UK: An Introduction*. London: Routledge.

Smith, R. G. (2014). Responding to Organised Crime Through Intervention in Recruitment Pathways. *Trends and Issues in Crime and Criminal Justice, 473*, 1.

Sproat, P. (2009). To What Extent Is the UK's Anti-Money Laundering and Asset Recovery Regime Used Against Organised Crime? *Journal of Money Laundering Control, 12*(2), 134–150.

Sproat, P. (2012). Phoney War or Appeasement? The Policing of Organised Crime in the UK. *Trends in Organized Crime, 15*, 313–330. https://doi.org/10.1007/s12117-012-9154-4.

SRA. (2014). *Cleaning Up: Law Firms and the Risk of Money Laundering*. Solicitor's Regulation Authority. Available at: http://www.sra.org.uk/risk/resources/risk-money-laundering.page

Stelfox, P. (1998). Policing Lower Levels of Organised Crime in England and Wales. *The Howard Journal, 37*(4), 393–406.

Thrasher, F. M. (1927). *The Gang*. Chicago/London: University of Chicago Press.

UK Government Legislation. (2017). Fraud Act 2006. *legislation.gov.uk* [Online]. Available at: http://www.legislation.gov.uk/ukpga/2006/35/crossheading/fraud. Accessed 10 May 2017.

UK Parliament. (2017). Criminal Finances Act 2017. *www.parliament.uk* [Online]. Available at: http://services.parliament.uk/bills/2016-17/criminalfinances.html. Accessed 10 May 2017.

UNODC. (2002). *Results of a Pilot Survey of Forty Selected Organized Criminal Groups in Sixteen Countries*. Global Programme Against Transnational Organized Crime. United Nations Office on Drugs and Crime.

van Dijck, M. (2007). Discussing Definitions of Organised Crime: Word Play in Academic and Political Discourse. *HUMSEC Journal, 1*(1), 65–90.

van Duyne, P. C. (1996). *Organised Crime in Europe*. New York: Nova Science Publishers Inc.

van Duyne, P. C., von Lampe, K., and Passas, N. (Eds.). (2002). *Upperworld and Underworld in Cross-Border Crime*. Nijmegen: Wolf Legal Publishers.

van Koppen, M. and De Poot, C. (2013). The Truck Driver Who Bought a Café: Offenders in Their Involvement Mechanisms for Organized Crime. *European Journal of Criminology, 10*(1), 74–88.

van Koppen, M., De Poot, C., Kleemans, E., and Nieuwbeerta, P. (2010). Criminal Trajectories in Organized Crime. *British Journal of Criminology, 50*, 102–123.

von Lampe, K. (2014). *Definitions of Organized Crime*. http://www.organized-crime.de/index.html

von Lampe, K. (2015). *Organized Crime: Analyzing Illegal Activities, Criminal Structures, and Extra-Legal Governance*. Los Angeles: Sage Publications.

von Lampe, K. (2017). http://www.organized-crime.de/index.html. Latest update 7 February 2017. Accessed 11 Apr 2017.

Wall, D. S. (2015). The Internet as a Conduit for Criminals. In A. Pattavina (Ed.), *Information Technology and the Criminal Justice System* (pp. 77–98). Thousand Oaks: Sage.

Wilson, G. and Wilson, S. (2007). Can the General Fraud Offence 'Get the Law Right'?: Some Perspectives on the 'Problem' of Financial Crime. *The Journal of Criminal Law, 71*(1), 36–53.

Wolfe, D. T. and Hermanson, D. R. (2004). The Fraud Diamond: Considering the Four Elements of Fraud. *The CPA Journal, 74*(12), 38.

World Economic Forum. (2012). *Organised Crime Enablers: Global Agenda Council on Organized Crime*. World Economic Forum. Available at: http://reports.weforum.org/organized-crime-enablers-2012/

Wright, A. (2006). *Organised Crime*. Cullompton: Willan.

Notes

1. The anonymised extract excluded six percent of OCGs (and 6203 nominals) some of which included groups originating from Police Scotland. However, it is possible that Scottish OCGs not investigated by Police Scotland appeared in the extract provided for this analysis.
2. The most common types of economic crime reported to the OCGM were 'non-fiscal (tax) fraud' (n = 422); 'public sector fraud, business tax fraud/evasion (including MTIC fraud)' (n = 218); 'public sector fraud, personal tax fraud/evasion (including income tax/self-assessment fraud)' (n = 213); 'banking and credit fraud, mortgage fraud' (n = 199); 'public sector fraud, excise/customs duty fraud (including tobacco/alcohol fraud, fuel/oil fraud, illegal gambling)' (n = 189); 'identity theft' (n = 184); 'public sector fraud, benefit fraud (non-tax credit /repayment fraud)' (n = 166); 'banking and credit fraud, account takeover' (n = 156); 'insurance fraud' (n = 150); and 'payment card crime' (n = 120).
3. This included offences reported to the OCGM relating to 'fraudulently obtained genuine (FOG) documentation—supply or use in organised immigration crime' (n = 104), counterfeit currency (any involvement) (n = 76), 'intellectual property' offences (n = 70), and 'human trafficking to exploit state benefits (age group unknown)' (n = 49), or involving adults (n = 41) and juveniles (n = 13).
4. Details of these groups engaged in high levels of fraud-related activity were submitted by 11 (of 12) reporting regions, but with 93% originating from an organisation with a national remit (61.7%—typically HMRC—n = 126) and London (30.8%). There were, however, some important differences between the high criminality fraud groups submitted to OCGM by the various reporting agencies. Those groups submitted by HMRC, for example, were more likely to have extenuating factors reported (55%) than fraud-related OCGs submitted by other organisations (21%). This was true in relation to exceptional levels of criminality, having high impact enabling activity and unassessed criminality. By contrast, those fraud-related OCGs reported by HMRC as being engaged in this criminality to a high level had

a smaller percentage of groups with extenuating factors linked to exceptional community impact and a high level of political and/or reputational damage arising from their activities. While these differences will to a large extent simply reflect what was known about the characteristics and features of the groups concerned, it is important to acknowledge that these profiles will also be influenced by the way in which individual agencies process, interpret, and grade the intelligence they have on OCGs.

5. These other fraud groups were submitted from across the 12 reporting regions and sources, but with around two-thirds (64.5%) originating from an agency with a national remit (44.7%—most commonly HMRC—n = 170) and London (19.8%).
6. In addition to chi-square (χ^2) tests, which were run to examine the null hypothesis that the distributions of categorical variables were the same across groups, Student's t-tests or one-way analysis of variance (ANOVA), as appropriate, were undertaken to assess whether mean observations within continuous/numeric data were significantly different. Correlation analysis sought to identify linear relationships between criminality types. Finally, univariate and multiple logistic regression analyses were used to explore which factors best predicted involvement in a high level of organised fraud-related criminality.
7. Standard deviation.
8. Adjustments were made for multiple testing within all ANOVA analyses using the Bonferroni correction (i.e. $\alpha = 0.05$/number of tests).
9. The National Crime Agency advises caution when interpreting data on the extent to which criminality is considered to be Internet/technology enabled due to underreporting. These questions were also not contained within the original version of the tracker.
10. In the first instance, univariate logistic regression analyses were undertaken involving each of the independent predictor variables to assess their suitability for inclusion in multivariate analysis. Significance levels of $p < 0.10$ were used as a cut-off point for univariate analysis and multivariate inclusion criteria. The results of the univariate regression analyses are shown in Appendix 2. At a univariate level, all of the factors examined were found to be significantly predictive of involvement in a high level of fraud-related criminality. Once identified as appropriate for inclusion, each of the predictor variables was entered into the multivariate model (on the basis of their respective p-values and Wald statistic). These factors explained 41% of the variance in involvement in a high level of organised fraud-related criminality ($R^2 = 0.407$) and correctly classified 91% of the cases. The small chi-square value ($\chi^2(8) = 4.1$) and high corresponding p-value ($p = 0.852$) indicated a good fit for this particular model. Using a backward elimination approach to sequentially remove those factors with high p-values, a further eight iterations of the model did not adversely impact upon the chi-square

value of the Hosmer and Lemeshow test ($\chi^2(8) = 4.3$) or its associated *p*-value ($p = 0.828$), again indicating a good fit for these data. Removing these eight factors from the model also had no significant impact on the relevant log-likelihood (*-2LL*) value (from 573.2 to 578.6), Nagelkerke R-squared statistic ($R^2 = 0.400$), or the extent to which cases were correctly classified (91%). Model iterations were as follows: Removed first iteration: has at least one specialist role ($p = 0.970$). Removed second iteration: intent and capability: cash flow ($p = 0.839$). Removed third iteration: impacts upon a community to an exceptional level ($p = 0.808$). Removed fourth iteration: intent and capability: resistance/resilience ($p = 0.707$). Removed fifth iteration: intent and capability: infiltration, corruption, and subversion ($p = 0.457$). Removed sixth iteration: the group has a recognised structure ($p = 0.390$). Removed seventh iteration: any areas of criminality flagged on OCGM as Internet/technology enabled ($p = 0.222$). Removed eighth iteration: intent and capability: expertise ($p = 0.128$).

Index[1]

[1] Note: Page numbers followed by 'n' refer to notes.

T. May, B. Bhardwa, *Organised Crime Groups involved in Fraud*,
Crime Prevention and Security Management,
https://doi.org/10.1007/978-3-319-69401-6

CPSIA information can be obtained
at www.ICGtesting.com
Printed in the USA
LVHW03*2001090918
589617LV00006B/250/P

9 783319 694009